DANCING GABE

DANCING GABE

ONE STEP AT A TIME

DANIEL PERRON

Foreword by Mark Chipman
Executive Chairman of the Board of True North Sports & Entertainment Limited and Winnipeg Jets Hockey Club

Published by Daniel Perron & Associates

Library and Archives Canada Cataloguing in Publication

Perron, Daniel
Dancing Gabe: one step at a time / Daniel Perron
978-0-9948081-0-3 (Hard Cover)
978-0-9948081-1-0 (Soft Cover)
978-0-9948081-2-7 (eBook)

Published by Daniel Perron & Associates
Winnipeg, MB R3Y 1K4
danielperron.dpa@gmail.com

Cover photo by Mike Sudoma, Mike Sudoma Photography, Winnipeg, MB
Lindor Reynolds' quote on the front cover from the *Winnipeg Free Press*, Saturday, October 24, 1992. Lindor Reynolds, The Other Side column "At games, he grooves," page D1. Reproduced with permission.

Book design and production by Relish New Brand Experience Inc.
Editing by Byron Rempel-Burkholder
Chapter opening photos courtesy of the Langlois family or by the author
Author photograph by Diana dela Cruz, Diana dela Cruz Photography, Winnipeg, MB

Printed in Canada by Friesens, Altona, MB

To Angélina Langlois

TABLE OF CONTENTS

FOREWORD

I'm not sure when I first encountered Gabe Langlois and his infectious smile but it must have been during a break in the action at a Winnipeg Jets game in the mid-1990's. Our seats were in the southwest corner of the old Winnipeg Arena, just above an opening from the concourse, a perfect perch for Gabe to display his enthusiasm.

Those were gut-wrenching days for Winnipeg Jets fans. We knew something had to give and despite everyone's best efforts, in the spring of 1996, the bottom fell out of our NHL run. Our city's psyche took a beating, probably more so than anyone could have imagined. But then as Manitobans so often do, we picked ourselves up, strengthened our resolve and moved on. No better example of that spirit was Gabe Langlois.

That summer we concluded the purchase of the Manitoba Moose. When we began play in the fall, I don't think anyone, myself included, knew what the reaction would be. We had literally had our hearts ripped out just months earlier and now people were being asked to watch the Las Vegas Thunder instead of the Montreal Canadiens.

I don't remember much about that first home game other than we lost to Vegas 1-0 and that Dancing Gabe Langlois was there in a Moose jersey like nothing else had happened in the months leading up to our move to the IHL.

For many, the Moose would never be good enough and were just a painful reminder of what we had lost. None of that mattered to Gabe. He embraced us and I distinctly remember how good that felt because for Gabe, it's never been about which league we played in, it has always just been about his unblemished sense of loyalty to the home team and his love of our community.

For the following fifteen years, Gabe was a fixture at Moose games. You could count on one hand the number of games he and I missed. It wasn't the NHL, but it was to me and it was to Gabe. Though I got better at managing my emotions during the Moose era, I would live and die during those games, Gabe just lived and it was often his unshakable optimism that I would look to during a time-out.

The story of our return to the NHL is well documented and I could fill up several pages trying to explain how and why it came to be. But this is a story about Gabe Langlois and how his life makes what we do simply better.

Beneath all the glamour and excitement that is the NHL, lies a very challenging, complex business where your every move is scrutinized and perhaps deservedly so. Someone once said that Canada is a country of thirty million General Managers. No truer words were ever spoken, except Gabe isn't one of them. Gabe is a fan in the truest sense of the word. He loves his teams and there is a purity in that which causes my heart to swell.

That honesty of spirit, it seems to me, is so foreign these days and I can't help but wonder how much better off we would be if we all possessed just a fraction of what Gabe brings to the table.

Our goal is to win a Stanley Cup and every time we see another team hoist it in June our resolve is strengthened. I can't imagine how our community would respond. I think about Gabe and how fired up he would be as well, but I am also reminded that Dancin' Gabe will be behind us no matter what comes our way. That reality is a blessing I'm thankful for every time I walk in the rink.

—Mark Chipman, Executive Chairman of the Board of True North Sports & Entertainment Limited and Winnipeg Jets Hockey Club

PREFACE

Before I began researching for this book, I knew less about Gabriel Langlois than did most sports fans in Winnipeg. I had read Gordon Sinclair's and Geoff Kirbyson's articles about him in the *Winnipeg Free Press* and caught the wave of respect and affection people have for this beloved 52-year-old fan. I had seen "Dancing Gabe" at every game I had attended, whether of the Winnipeg Goldeyes, Jets, or Blue Bombers. How could anyone miss his six-foot tall, 250-pound frame, dancing in the aisles! But I had yet to really encounter him.

In July 2014, when Gabe's brother Michel asked me to write Gabe's biography, I thought I would focus mostly on his role on Game Day, as an ever-present cheerleader, dancing to the music between plays, and whipping up the enthusiasm of the crowds. However, I would soon discover that Gabe's life story is composed of many more interesting, dramatic, and touching aspects that put Game Day in perspective.

More than a hundred interviews, trips to Winnipeg's Centennial Library, the Centre du Patrimoine in St. Boniface, Treherne, Notre-Dame-de Lourdes, Portage la Prairie, and enjoyable afternoons spent with Gabe and his mom, Angélina, helped me uncover the details of Dancing Gabe's journey and get to know the many wonderful people who contributed to it. People who greeted a stranger with open arms and welcomed the opportunity to talk about Gabe and contribute to the project. They sent me on many trails that would reinforce the saying, "There's only one degree of separation in Manitoba."

Finally, Gabe granted me access to two of his own collections as a primary source: the scrapbooks he has kept over the years (see sidebar)

GABE'S SCRAPBOOK COLLECTION

Over the last thirty years, Gabe painstakingly assembled a collection of forty-five scrapbooks—more than 3,000 pages—chronicling Winnipeg's most noteworthy sporting events. The books contain news clippings, game tickets, autograph pages, program pages, and special events commemoration, posters, dinner menus (one from the 1997 Manitoba Moose Yearling Foundation Dinner), photographs, statistics, and stickers. Many pages are devoted to the 1990s fight to keep the Jets from leaving Winnipeg, and one even includes a bronze commemorative key chain replica of the ticket for the Jets last regular season game—L.A. Kings vs Jets, Friday, April 12, 1996.

Hundreds of yellow PostIt notes affixed by Gabe stick out of the books, marking every article that mentions Dancing Gabe, simplified my research.

and his scribbler, often quoted in the book, which his mother helped him compile as a record of his early life experiences.

A brief note about my process: Many of the quoted conversations, especially earlier ones (for example, encounters at the doctor's office), are composites, pieced together and reimagined on the basis of the recollections of the speakers. As for the language used for mental health and disabilities, I chose to retain the language as it was used at the time, in the papers, in reports, and in conversations. It demonstrates how far we have come as a community in this domain.

Gabe's early years were difficult, very difficult. He was born with an intellectual disability that would be diagnosed as autism by the time he turned four. The demands of Gabe's condition, which at the time was still poorly understood, stretched his parents' resolve to its breaking point. Giving up on Gabe and sending him away to an institution may have seemed like the only option at times.

Fortunately, giving up was not in the vocabulary of Angélina, Gabe's mother: her son was a part of the family—a part of her. Gabe's sister and four brothers also accepted him for the brother he was, along with his disability. They looked out for him, as many others did, loved him, and allowed him to grow, to develop and to follow his very own path. Gabriel Langlois' life is a story of love—the unconditional love of a family and the strength of its bonds.

Sister Alice Konefall, principal at Holy Cross School when Gabe attended there, spoke of the family's courage. "You know the root of the word courage, yes?" she asked me. "You should, it is a good French word, meaning *agir avec coeur* (acting with heart), with conviction. Gabriel is a fine example of courage, as is his mother."

Courage, resolve, patience, and perseverance would be essential in raising Gabe to overcome the challenges his autism presented. Popular culture, over the past thirty years, has shed light on autism and related intellectual disabilities. Movies like *Rainman*, *A Beautiful Mind*, *Awakenings*, *Radio*, and *Temple Grandin*, along with books like *A Curious Incident of the Dog in the Night* have provided a first-hand look at the challenges of living with mental disabilities, thus helping us understand them better.

The story of "Dancing Gabe" Langlois, son of Angélina and Louis, offers us a fuller, more intimate picture of someone we feel we know already, a window into the way ordinary families like his deal with autism in their everyday lives. In these pages you will see an example of a person who, along with his family, let nothing stand in the way of building and living a life that is full and satisfying. For Gabe, and for his mother, coping would prove difficult, initially. However, coping would not be enough. Thrive he must, and he did.

Gabe's life story is similar to our own in many ways. The stories of our lives resemble icebergs: for the most part, they lie below the surface, their riches remaining to be discovered through the effort of telling them. Gabe's iceberg reveals stunning colours, melodic sounds, intricate series of events, and heart-warming people. The crevasses hide tears, pain, sorrow, joy, hope, happiness, faith, love, family, friendship, caring, pride, passion, and selflessness.

According to the old African proverb, it takes a village to raise a child. In the case of Gabriel Langlois, it has taken several "villages"—his family, friends, teachers, classmates, neighbours, staff in Portage la

Prairie, foster parents in Notre-Dame-de-Lourdes, sports teams, and tens of thousands of Winnipeg sports fans. Each of these communities has formed an integral part of Gabe's journey.

Allow me to tell you about Gabriel Langlois' iceberg: some parts you will already know; many you will not. Most will amaze you.

—*Daniel Perron, Winnipeg, 2015*

FIRST HALF COPING

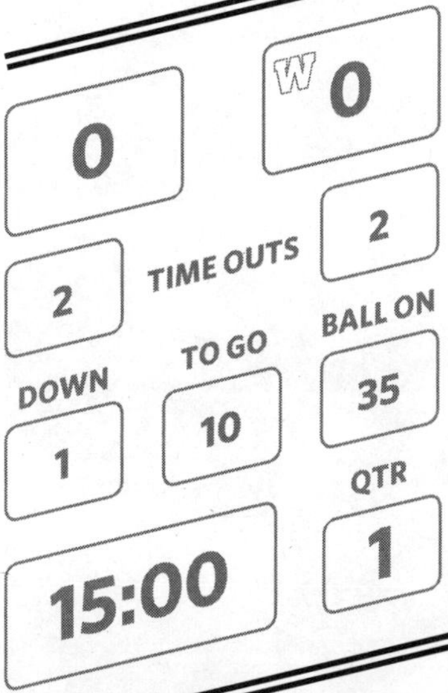

FIRST QUARTER

MEET DANCING GABE

91
W

CHAPTER 1

Game Day

> Those who were seen dancing were thought to be insane by those who could not hear the music.
>
> —*Henri-Louis Bergson*[1]

Thursday, August 7, 2014

For Gabriel "Dancing Gabe" Langlois, one third of his calendar consists of game days, with an average of 105 professional sports regular season home games every year. Pre-season games, playoff games, university and amateur sports, and community events fill the rest of his busy schedule. Not to mention bowling, working, working out, and volunteering.

Today's game pits the Winnipeg Blue Bombers against the defending Grey Cup champs, the Saskatchewan Roughriders. The contest will write another page in the long story of the bitter rivalry between these two teams.

"I got up around 7:00. I did nothing special, really," says Gabe.

His game day breakfast consists of Weetabix cereal—he calls this his "Bix Fix,"—with creamy peanut butter and toast, and coffee with two creams and no sugar. Then he reads the day's *Winnipeg Free Press*, as he does every day of the year. He reads every line of the Sports section and leafs through the rest of the paper. He also scans the *Winnipeg Sun*.

His weekday mornings are spent at the South YMCA on Fermor Avenue, next door to his alma mater, Glenlawn Collegiate, and only a few minutes' walk from his house on Hull Avenue. There, he works and works out. He enjoys his time there, but the real excitement is yet to come.

> "Reality to an autistic person is a confusing interacting mass of events, people, places, sounds, and sights. ... A large part of my life is spent just trying to work out the patterns behind everything. Set routines, time, particular routes, and rituals all help to get order into an unbearably chaotic life."[2]
>
> —*Temple Grandin, in* Thinking in Pictures

He is home by 1:00 p.m. for a quick snack, before gearing up for the game, something he does on more than 200 days each year.

Today, after finishing in a flash his late-afternoon pre-game meal of rotini pasta (his mom usually prepares fettuccine Alfredo, but Gabe takes this change in stride), he soon retires to his room, in the basement, and readies himself for the game. Entering Gabe's room, painted blue and gold, feels like walking into a Winnipeg sports shrine: a twin bed with its Jets bedspread; two dressers covered with sports artifacts and trophies; two small shelves bow under the weight of bobble-heads, pucks, and coffee mugs; three walls where autographed pictures, posters, flags, and a goalie mask hang; one television. One wall bucks the trend, plain white, with a folding curtain, which Gabe opens to reveal its contents.

Gabe owns quite the collection of jerseys—twenty-nine in all, (thirty including the recent acquisition of a genuine Jets Whiteout jersey for the 2015 playoffs)—neatly arranged in his closet. They range from early edition Blue Bombers jerseys and personalized Goldeyes jerseys to a variety of Winnipeg Jets jerseys. One bears the name "Warren's Corner Sports," a present for Gabe. Another, a Manitoba Moose jersey, is adorned with the red and black Wise Guys logo on the back—a popular bar and grill that adopted Dancing Gabe to its family.

Dancing Gabe emerges in his 2012 Edition Blue Bombers No. 91 jersey with his stage name on the back, his Investors Group Field (IGF) pass around his neck, his hair gelled and slicked back.

"Number 91," he explains, "because that's the year when I became Dancing Gabe, officially."

Gabe looks at the clock. It's four o'clock, time for him to catch the bus to the game.

"I usually take the 14 to Bishop Grandin (St. Mary's South), then the 75/76 or the 51," he says. "It only takes me thirty minutes to get to IGF." Sometimes he gets a ride, but most days he uses his monthly bus pass. He has memorized his bus schedules.

The temperature is a muggy 29 degrees Celsius, ideal for an evening football game.

We reach a busy St. Mary's Road; it is rush hour. Gabe waves at me before crossing the thoroughfare's northbound lanes, toward the boulevard.

"Look both ways, Gabe!" I yell, like a nervous parent.

My voice is drowned out by the deafening and constant engine and tire noise. I wave back—half wave, half warning signal.

Gabe makes it onto the boulevard, halfway to the safety of the ad-covered bench at the bus stop. He gauges the southbound traffic. A driver in the inside lane stops to let him cross. Cars in the outside lane are still zooming by, but they, too, come to a stop as Gabe ventures off the boulevard.

He catches my eye as he gets to the bus stop, smiles broadly, and waves goodbye. My heart is still in my throat. I wonder why he doesn't use the crosswalk a mere hundred feet south.

I smile and wave back and turn my camera on just in time to photograph the puff of blue smoke from the exhaust pipe of the southbound Winnipeg Transit number 14 bus, as it speeds away, its precious cargo

safely seated. It is Game Day, and Dancing Gabe has a rendezvous for some serious Roughriders butt-kickin'... and a lot of dancin'.

Launch of a sports fan career

As I saw Gabe off to the game, I couldn't help but think about how far he had come in thirty years. The first day of summer 1984 was the first day of Gabe's career as a true sports fan. It was the day he attended his first CFL game, a pre-season contest between the Blue Bombers and the B.C. Lions. Gabe remembers it as if it was yesterday. A low scoring game that saw the Lions defeat the Bombers by a score of 13–4 in front of a crowd of 24,809 brave, wet, and disappointed fans.

"There were big thunderstorms: thunder, lightning, deluge, a major downpour. So the game was delayed," he says. "The Red River Ex was in town!"

Seems it always pours when the Ex is in town, ha!

Gabe is not classified as a savant[3]—the few people with an autism spectrum disorder (ASD) who can memorize the names of every street in a city, or every book in the library. But anyone who interacts with Gabe is impressed by his ability to recall facts, dates, scores, records, and players' names and numbers with disconcerting ease and the utmost confidence. Gabe knows every stop on his bus routes and most sport records in the *Guinness Book of World Records*, which he buys every year.

A look at the Blue Bombers website confirms the accuracy of Gabe's recollection of his first game in 1984. Game-time weather indicates "thunderstorms, heavy rain showers, and moderate hail, with winds from the west at thirty kilometres per hour."

That same summer, on July 8, Gabe saw his first regular season game, when the Blue Bombers played the Toronto Argonauts. "I bought my own ticket and took the bus all by myself to what was then the Winnipeg Stadium," Gabe recalls.

The excitement of the game energized Gabe and soon he was up, dancing, cheering, and encouraging fans around him to cheer along.

Gabe enjoyed this rush of new emotions; he felt really good. His contagious enthusiasm spread to the fans around him, their response fuelling Gabe, and he kept on dancing. The Blue Bombers defeated the Argos by a score of 26 to 24. In Gabe's words, it was "winning ugly," but a win nevertheless.

That year, he watched the western final game on television. Gabe recalls that the Bombers defeated the B.C. Lions 32–14, to earn a berth in the Grey Cup against Hamilton and then go on to hoist their first Grey Cup after a twenty-two year drought.

Gabe also remembers the stars of that game: Tom Clements at quarterback, Willard Reeves, Joe Poplawski, Chris Walby, and Lyle Bauer. It was Lyle Bauer who, more than fifteen years later as the Blue Bombers president and chief executive officer, recognized that Dancing Gabe was a "feel good" story and deserved some more attention. According to Bombers employee at the time, Kate Gameiro, that's when Gabe was granted "all access" to Bomber games.

Dancing up a storm at Investors Group Field

Friday, August 22, 2014

Getting to the bus stop on this day is much less stressful than my first experience with Gabe catching the bus. We cross St. Mary's together, but still don't use the crosswalk. While we sit on the bench, waiting for the number 14 bus, cars beep their horns, passengers roll down their windows and call, "Hey Dancing Gabe," "Hey Gabe!" or "You rock Gabe!" I feel like I am sitting beside a rock star. After a short while, a large man in a white Hummer stops and waves. "Hey, Gabe!"

Gabe walks over. The two converse for a few seconds, and then Gabe turns and waves me over. "We've got a ride!"

The driver, whose size makes the Hummer feel small, introduces himself as Cory McDiarmid, the Bombers linebackers' coach.

At the stadium, the atmosphere is charged with excitement as fans gather for tailgate parties and mill around the entrances. Gabe walks into the Bombers store, which is well stocked and already buzzing with activity. Customers and staff are glad to see him. Bombers CEO Wade Miller is in the middle of a conversation but waves at him.

Tara Maslowsky, Account Executive for Ticketing, greets Gabe and ushers him to the main counter where she draws Gabe's attention to the new jerseys hanging from the ceiling.

"It's their Signature jersey," Gabe tells me.

The jersey design is a departure from what fans are used to: what almost looks like military camouflage in various shades of blue but with no traditional gold. A completely new look.

In less time than it takes Bombers quarterback Drew Willy to call an audible, Gabe is out of his traditional blue and gold jersey and into his own Signature Blue Bomber jersey with his name and his number, 91, emblazoned on the back. Other staff congregate around him to voice their approval. Gabe is beaming.

Tara Maslowsky and Dancing Gabe

"When we put on autograph signing promos, he's always first in line. We don't have to call him and we know we can count on Gabe. Gabe has brand recognition."

—*Tara Maslowsky, Bombers Account Executive, Ticketing*

Gabe now steps outside and wanders through the festive promotional events that precede the opening of the gates. Lush green grass is covered with marquee tents and buzzing with expectant fans. Cheerleading teams build their human pyramids one minute and disassemble them the next, to the rhythm of the booming music.

Fans approach Gabe, one hand in the air, palm open and fingers extended as Gabe does the same. They high-five, exchange greetings and continue on their way, smiling. A few stop for a quick chat.

As the gates open, Gabe is greeted by Bombers staff, media personalities, and others eager to say hi, shake his hand or high-five Gabe. He is in his element; this is his stage.

The Reebok representative approaches, hands Gabe an iPad, and asks him to fill out a questionnaire. Gabe takes on a serious look, focuses on the tablet, and completes the questionnaire before finding his own season's ticket assigned seat: Section 118, Row 2, Seat 5. He puts his bag down, looks around, and scouts out the scene. Everyone is busy putting the finishing touches before the throngs of fans arrive.

After crunching through a large bag of popcorn—no butter—Gabe saunters down the stairs to the edge of the field, where players from both teams are warming up, stretching, tossing the football, running routes. Sara Orleski, the TSN sports reporter, walks over, smiles, and shakes Gabe's hand. They chat for a minute. Gabe is proud to show off his new Bomber jersey. The Blue Bomber Cheer Team waves at him, a wave he gladly returns with a broad smile. This feels like one big family reunion.

Gabe is being watched closely as he completes a questionnaire

Mason, a blond-haired boy with the ball cap, peak backwards, approaches from the front row. "Hi Dancing Gabe! Can I take a selfie with you?" Gabe is only too happy to oblige. They both examine the result on Mason's phone and nod in approval. A handshake, smiles for everyone, and Gabe is on his way. His young fan returns to his seat, eager to show his prize picture to his awaiting friends.

The scene will repeat itself all evening. A fan walks over, cell phone in hand. There's a high-five or a handshake, a brief exchange, smiles, laughter. Then the fan puts an arm around Gabe's shoulders, extends the phone at arm's length, smiles, and clicks. The souvenir will be shared with friends and family on Facebook, Twitter, Instagram, or Pinterest.

The expressions of intrigue on the faces of people watching Dancing Gabe are no surprise. Here he is, a fifty-one-year-old, garbed in custom glare guard eye-black strips, blue and gold shorts, his own Signature jersey (How did he get that? they must wonder), and size 13 Blue Bombers cross trainers (a present from former Bombers marketing director Jeffrey Bannon)—strutting, dancing, and cheering up and down the stadium's stairs, shaking his pompoms. His energy remains constant from the opening kickoff until the game's final seconds.

As the kickoff moment approaches, Bombers mascots Buzz and Boomer enter the field, waving to the cheering crowd. Next comes the pirouetting and tumbling Blue Bombers Cheer Team. Captain Blue buzzes noisily around the field (with the bi-plane's wheels safely on the ground, of course), waving at the fans, his flying helmet and goggles anchored on his head and his long yellow scarf floating behind him like a flag in a Winnipeg windstorm. He comes to a full stop at centre field, pulls himself out of the cockpit, steps on the seat, and salutes the crowd, who responds with a loud ovation.

The game is on.

"Gabe's got phenomenal dance moves! But the thing that impresses me the most is that he always remembers our name. He's an all-around great guy and he means a lot to the organization. For me, he's a friendly face who is a great ambassador for the team."

—Maria Todd, Bomber Store Assistant Manager

"The best part of going to the games is the atmosphere! ...I love meeting the people, the fans. I go crazy. I go out and cheer! Win, lose or tie, it doesn't matter."

—Gabe

Keeping up with the Bombers' number one fan suddenly turns into a monumental task. Gabe covers the entire lower bowl twice during the game, making his way up and down every aisle. Between plays, he dances to the music booming from the field's massive sound system; when play resumes he finds an empty seat, sits down, and watches attentively.

Just before the end of the second quarter, an usher with a blue mustache introduces Gabe to a gentleman and his wife, daughter, and granddaughters in their special section. The "Gabe effect" is immediate: high-fives, handshakes, smiles, and a souvenir photo.

After chatting for a minute or so, Gabe bids them farewell; he has an appointment at the snack bar, as he does during every game, before the half-time rush. By the time the seconds tick down to zero on the game clock, Gabe carries his box of chicken fingers and fries, ready to sit down and enjoy.

The teams return and warm up while Buzz and Boomer amuse the crowd. Buzz spots Dancing Gabe and walks over, waving. Fans notice that the scene is captured on the giant screen: Buzz gives a low bow salute to Dancing Gabe, which he returns ceremoniously, to the loud cheers of thirty thousand fans.

In the second half of the game, the handshakes and photo ops pick up. A young woman stands up, puts her arm around Gabe and nestles her head on his shoulder as her boyfriend snaps the picture. Gabe has

> "You can't always count on the teams to win, but you can always count on Gabe. He is always professional and respectful. People like him because he's real."
>
> —*Kevin, veteran usher with the blue mustache*

not cleared the aisle yet when another fan stands up to greet him with a bright smile.

"A picture, please?" she asks.

"Sure!" is Gabe's standard answer. Gabe puts his arm around the young woman's shoulders, as she leans over, delighted. She gives a thumbs-up, holding a black and gold Michael Kors clutch. The flash shines once, twice. She thanks Gabe with a big hug. He smiles, thanks her, and continues his tireless walk, proceeding to the next section.

Fans clap and cheer him on, and some get up and dance with him. A joy gleams from each of these brief encounters, like rays of sunshine. A mutual thank you. The response of the fans makes it all worthwhile for Dancing Gabe: exciting, electric!

After a slow first half that ended in a 6–1 score, the pace picks up in the second half. During the Alouettes' first play sequence, Winnipeg blocks a punt and returns it for a touchdown. The crowd goes nuts. The lead changes hands until the last two minutes of the game, when the Bombers cap a scoring drive with their third touchdown of the game. Ample time remains for the Alouettes to mount a final drive and challenge the Bombers' lead, but a timely interception puts the final exclamation mark on a superb evening of football, as Winnipeg defeats Montreal 24 to 16.

RELISHING THE GLORY, DEFLECTING THE INSULTS

Over the years, Gabe has been hit by his share of flying peanuts, and some inconsiderate or inebriated fans have even tripped him in his journeys up and down stadium and arena stairs. Angélina remembers the freezing cold Grey Cup game in 1991, when someone stole his favourite hat, covered in pins he had collected over the years. Years later, at the Grey Cup in Toronto, a Saskatchewan fan called Gabe a "retard."[4] These insults never hurt Gabe, at least on the outside; he accepts that people might say stupid things that they regret later, usually after they drink too much...

But they soon learn that Gabe's fan support runs very deep. Fans have come to Gabe's rescue on a number of occasions, making it necessary for security staff to intervene to protect his tormentors. Funny how that works.

> "People should know that he's a Winnipeg icon, but it's more than just that. Also he's so kind. I don't think I've ever met someone as kind and thoughtful as him. He's probably experienced more discrimination than many, but the way he deals with it is remarkable."
>
> —*Stephanie Blandford, Gabe's dance partner on* Dancing With Celebrities

---

Gabe's fan support became apparent in 2007 when *Winnipeg Free Press* columnist Gordon Sinclair Jr., inspired by readers Bob and Sandra, organized a fundraising campaign to send Dancing Gabe and his brother Rick to the 2007 Grey Cup in Toronto. Scott Neiles of Home Run Sports paid for the tickets to the game, WestJet covered the airfare, and the Winnipeg Fairmont covered part of the accommodations. Spending money came from hundreds of fans. The trip was what Gordon Sinclair, Jr., called "a dream come true" for Gabe.[5]

The excitement isn't over yet for Gabe. "We're looking for bus 75," he says as we start walking toward the street, where thousands of fans are filing onto hundreds of Winnipeg Transit and school buses. Gabe walks with a hurried pace and a determined look on his face. He has obviously done this many times before.

He finds bus 75 and heads straight for the door. He does not seem to notice the line of passengers extending a few hundred feet from the door, but nobody seems to object. Moments later, our bus makes its way out of the University of Manitoba campus.

Back at Hull Avenue, I invite Gabe for a coffee and a doughnut at Tim Horton's.

"Can we bring one for my Mom?" he asks.

GABE'S DANCING BY THE NUMBERS—FOOTBALL

Since he started dancing in stadium aisles in 1984, Gabe attended a total of 305 Bombers home games at the old Canad Inns Stadium (formerly the Winnipeg Stadium). With its lower bowl's 24 sections and stairways, Gabe covered approximately 7,840 steps per game, for a total of 2,391,200 steps. At Investors Group Field (IGF), by the end of the 2014 season, Gabe attended a total of 20 games. With its lower bowl's 44 sections and stairways, Gabe covered approximately 8,448 steps per game, for a total of 168,960 steps.

For those counting, that means well over 2.5 million steps—the equivalent of walking from Winnipeg to Vancouver—just at football games! That's a lot of stepping plus a whole lotta shaking goin' on. But who's counting?

DANCING GABE
91

CHAPTER 2

What's Wrong with Little Gabe?

Autism is not a life sentence.

—*Glen Lowther, former Medical Superintendent, Manitoba School for Retardates*

I was born January 29, 1963, the month after the Winnipeg Blue Bombers won the 1962 Grey Cup. The Fog Bowl that is. I shared the same birthday with W.C. Fields, Ann Jillian, Oprah Winfrey, Domenic Hasek, Heather Graham, Johnny Lang, Gavin Walls. Yes! It's true, it's true. Lots of company.

I've come from a family. I am third (in the middle). I have four brothers and one sister: Mike, Rick, Rob, Gerry, and Claudette.

Mom gave birth to me at St. Boniface General Hospital. Baby number 3 in 1963! A boy!

Believe me! I was a winter baby, or what? I was born and raised in Winnipeg, Manitoba, Canada—the centre of North America. This is my life story... your truly.

Before I became the sports icon (a legend).

—Gabe's scribbler

"Having kids back then was the only break a mother would get," Angélina says with a chuckle. "I got to spend five days in hospital. A good holiday every year." She recalls that the temperature hovered around the –30 C mark when she brought Gabe home to their apartment on Burns Way (what is now Lagimodiere Boulevard).

Gabe was well behaved in those first weeks. He slept a lot and did not cry much. But Angélina was worried because he was so quiet. Fifty years later, the memory still brings tears to her eyes. “I couldn’t help but think that something just wasn’t right. He would not really make eye contact with the people around him, even when I talked to him. He would be *dans la lune* (in the moon) for long periods of time when he wasn’t sleeping.”

By the time Gabe should have been able to sit up, Angélina was pregnant with Rob, and caring for Mike and Rick. “I would put him in the high chair to feed him, but he would slouch and slump in the chair. Eventually, after Rob was born, I decided to take him to see Dr. Wiley, our family’s paediatrician, who then referred us to Dr. Ferguson at the Health Sciences Centre. It wasn’t easy to get four boys ready to go, to take the bus and make a couple of stops.”

At first Dr. Ferguson suspected spinal problems might be causing Gabe’s sitting difficulties. He even said that Gabe had “the bones of an old man.” Over several visits, he ruled out other causes.

Finally, in the summer of 1965, the doctor greeted Angélina with a concerned look. “Mrs. Langlois, I think we must come to the conclusion that Gabriel is mentally retarded. We need to consider the eventuality that Gabriel may never speak or walk”.

Retarded was the general term doctors used at the time to describe someone with significant impaired intellectual or adaptive functioning. The word echoed off the walls of the doctor’s office.

“I think I knew,” she remembers, “but I always hoped and prayed that I was wrong. Tears filled my eyes and I felt as if I had been punched in the stomach. The doctor handed me a tissue.”

After what seemed like an eternity, Angélina stood up, looked the doctor in the eye, and said, “I’m so nervous. Tell me the truth! Is he going to die?”

Dr. Ferguson reassured her that they should just try to take it one day at a time and make life as normal as possible for Gabe. After that visit, Angélina would visit the doctor twice a week until the end of summer and then once per month. Gabe’s diagnosis was a shock for his dad, Louis (who passed away in 1983). Ordinarily, Louis handled challenging situations well, but this proved to be a reality he found very difficult to accept.

"He didn't want to tell his family back in Ste. Flavie that he had a disabled child," Angélina recalls. "In those days, in many families, they sent kids like that to special places, away from everyone." Louis assumed, and possibly resigned himself, that this would be Gabe's fate.

In her many conversations with her husband, however, Angélina reaffirmed her goal of doing everything in her power to raise Gabe. She would ensure he grew up to live as normal a life as possible.

"Louis, you cannot hide a child, our child, a gift from God," Angélina recalls saying to her despondent husband.

In some ways, Gabe's growth was normal. Angélina breast fed Gabe until the summer of 1964, and then moved him on to formula and eventually normal food. He hated spinach and Brussels sprouts but loved broccoli, carrots, and mashed potatoes—anything mashed was good.

Gabe learned to walk at the age of eighteen months, which was also normal, but his autism made mobility a curse at times, since he would wander off (more on that in the next chapter).

Not normal, however, was the fact that he was nonverbal, and would not speak until he was nine. After Gabe turned three, Angélina spent a lot of time with him, sounding words and showing him objects and pictures associated with the words. He, in turn, would make sounds. Angélina would continue, almost certain that he was repeating the words she was telling him.

"I know he speaks!" she would tell Dr. McRae, the family doctor.

"You only think he does, Mrs. Langlois," he would reply.

Finally, the doctor agreed to admit Gabe at the Winnipeg Children's Hospital for three weeks of observation. The staff there would determine if his behaviour problem was associated with mental retardation. During his stay, the doctors prescribed the drug Chlorpromazine for aggressive and unmanageable behaviour. When he was discharged on January 24, 1966, the hospital report explained various aspects of his condition, and stated a diagnosis: "behaviour disorder—autism," known more commonly today as an autistic spectrum disorder (ASD).

Following Gabe's stay in the hospital, Angélina became discouraged over the Chlorpromazine medication. "I think it was a sedative," says Angélina, "because Gabe would fall asleep after taking it. He was so sleepy—I didn't want him sleeping all the time, that wasn't right—so I cut the dose in half."

Finally, Dr. McRae suggested placing Gabe in an institution, but Angélina would not hear of it, not for a minute.

Living with Gabe's autism

Most people in Winnipeg have heard of Dancing Gabe, seen him dance, or even met him. But few know of his disability; most simply think of him as a little "different." Gabe himself seldom mentions his disability, much less discusses it.

At the time of Gabe's diagnosis, autism was not a well understood disability; earlier in his life, his doctors had thought of it as "mental retardation." Autism, a lifelong condition, remains misunderstood by most people today, although research on it has advanced considerably. Today, the Autism Society Canada names autism as "the most common neurological disorder affecting children and one of the most common developmental disabilities affecting Canadians in general."[6]

ASD manifests itself in a variety of ways, which explains why it is called a *spectrum*. Some, like Gabe, live relatively independent lives, while others may have various learning disabilities and need a lifetime of specialist support. All people on the spectrum share a "triad of impairments" in areas of social communication, social interaction, and social imagination. The person with ASD may see life in pictures or patterns, often without emotion as we—people not on the spectrum—know them, taking things at face value, in a non-judgmental way.

"I actually forget about [Gabe's disability]. I don't hear people talk about it; they see him as who he is, as a person, first and foremost. This says a lot about who we are as a community, our spirit. He's one of us, one member of our community, and we support him."

—Brian Bowman, Winnipeg's Mayor

When asked about conversations with Gabe, Mike Langlois notes that his brother "doesn't process information quite the same way we do. You will need to ask very direct and specific questions. You will only get blank stares if you ask questions that are too vague or on a more abstract plane."

Many individuals with an ASD are either hypersensitive or hyposensitive to certain sounds, smells, touch, or other stimuli. Some exhibit nervous behaviours such as ticks, often in response to their frustration at their inability to do something, or to their parents' inability to understand their pain or discomfort.

Asked about Gabe's habit of fidgeting with his hands, Angélina explains, "He still does it when he's really bothered by something. But he's got it under control for the most part. When he was younger, if he was upset, he would rock, cry, and fidget with his hands, sometimes pretty wildly. Usually it was when he wanted something; maybe he saw someone get something—like a cookie—and he wanted one too."

"As a child he never liked noise and would put his hands over his ears whenever he heard any noise. He still does this and attempts to run into the next room. He also has a tendency to turn around in circles; he seems to enjoy this. In addition, he has very aggressive behaviour, running and climbing over everything. If he is thwarted, he throws himself on the floor and screams."

—Children's Hospital Discharge Summary, January 24, 1966

"I'll get you back!"

Despite everyone's efforts to rid Gabe of his fidgeting habit, this was Gabe's favourite escape as a child. He would walk around like an absent-minded professor, seemingly talking to himself, his head moving to-and-fro and his hands waving, as if leading the orchestra through a difficult movement of the symphony.

One story the family likes to tell dates back to when Gabe was eleven. From the living room, his little brother Gerry spotted Gabe on the sidewalk in front of the house. Some pedestrians would smile and point at him as they passed. Others would mock him and call him names. Others simply would ignore him.

This parade annoyed Gerry greatly. He opened the side door, took the stairs two at a time, and covered the distance to Gabe in an instant.

"Gabe, stop this nonsense with your hands! Why do you do this? People walk by and think you're nuts!"

Gabe continued his walk, waving his hands even more wildly. Gerry followed him.

"Stop that, Gabe! Don't you see that it's not normal?"

He reached for Gabe's hands, wanting to stop the movement, even if only for a few seconds. But Gabe resisted Gerry's hold and pulled away. In the scuffle, Gerry's hand accidentally whipped up to Gabe's face and knocked his glasses to the ground.

Gabe froze and looked down at his glasses, on the sidewalk, one lens shattered. Slowly, his gaze shifted to Gerry.

Angélina had observed the entire scene from her front window. Now, a smile spread across her lips as she watched Gerry take off down the street, Gabe in hot pursuit. She could hear Gabe yelling at Gerry.

"You just wait Gerry, I'll get you back one day!"

Angélina had no doubt that one day would come...

Seven years later, to the day, Gerry made his way painfully to the breakfast table, still feeling the effects of the night before, and sat down at his usual seat without saying a word. Claudette, Rob, Gabe, and Rick watched him pour a glass of orange juice while Angélina busied herself at the stove.

When Gabe finished his bowl of cereal, he got up and took his bowl to the sink. On his way back, he stood by Gerry. Gerry slowly looked up at his brother. Just then, Gabe surprised him with a solid right cross to the cheek. Everyone at the table, and Angélina at the stove, stopped and stared. They had never seen Gabe hit anyone, let alone his kid brother.

"I told you I would get you back one day. Well, I just did!" said Gabe.

"Are you going to hit me again?" asked Gerry, still groggy from the punch and rubbing his red cheek.

"No. I said I would get you, and I did. That's it!"

That was it. "*C'est la seule fois qu'il s'est fâché,*" recalls Angélina. "It's the only time he ever got mad, never mind hit someone."

WINNIPEG JETS
91

CHAPTER 3

La Petite Terreur

> The world of a nonverbal person with autism is chaotic and confusing.
> —*Temple Grandin,* Thinking in Pictures

La petite terreur (the little terror) is a term of endearment that Angélina Langlois uses often when referring to Gabe in his early years. She translates it "mischievous one," often comparing him to Dennis the Menace. From the age when he could walk, life with Gabe was filled with challenges to match the term—such as disappearances and dangerous episodes with fire. The fact that Gabe could not talk until he was nine complicated the functioning of family life and generated confusion for everyone around him.

The stresses would eventually lead to Gabe's five years away from home under the care of the Manitoba School for Retardates, including a stay with foster parents (see next chapter and following). However, the challenges of raising a child with autism did not deter his mother, nor would they dampen the affection he received from the rest of his family.

Angélina recalls vividly Gabe's mischievous moments and never tires of telling of them, with a smile. "He didn't do things with malice," she says, "but it was hard to keep up with him." This chapter offers a few windows into Gabe's early life in the context of his family:

Cake on the floor. Gabe was an early riser, according to his mom. "One day he went in the kitchen, took everything from the cupboard: flour, chocolate, porridge, sugar, and rolled oats. Then he took kids' clothes and boots. He picked a spot on the floor and mixed all the ingredients together and added milk and water."

The noise from the kitchen woke Angélina and Louis. "I got out of bed and Louis followed me. We both stopped dead in our tracks at the sight of this great mess. Gabe started to cry when he saw us," Angélina explains. "But Louis jumped right in and helped Gabe get the mix just right. That's just the way Louis loved to be with the kids; he was a kid at heart, himself."

Angélina gave Gabe a bath and then cleaned up the mess. "I knew it wasn't the last time I'd have to," she says with a grin.

Big brother Mike. From Gabe's scribbler: *My Mom had a big helper; it was Michel, my big brother. He was only three years older than me, but he was very good. He kept an eye on me while Mom ran downstairs to put the washing in the machine and then again when she had to go take the washing out of the machine. But first it was lunchtime, so she made sandwiches and Kool Aid. We went outside in the backyard to eat our lunch on the picnic table while my Mom would hang the clothes on the line.*

Paint job. From Gabe's scribbler: *One time I got out of the yard, walked in the back lane and saw an open garage door. In the garage there was this small car: a Corvette! But I did not like the colour green, so I looked around and saw some red and black paint on the shelf. So I decided to paint the Corvette red and black. I thought that was really nice. I turned around and in the doorway was a man. He did not say anything for a while, then he said, "I guess my car needed a paint job," just as my father came and didn't know what to say. I could tell he was not happy. I'm so sorry, but the mister was very understanding and said he would phone the insurance.*

Toilet training. Angélina tells of a stressful time for most parents: toilet training. "Gabe was in diapers until the age of five," the same age at which Gabe began uttering single words. "Toilet training was a real challenge for him—and for me. He would sit on the toilet for a long time but do nothing. He would get off the toilet... and then go in his pants. Then he would even smear it on the walls, which I would have to clean."

This compelled her to teach Gabe how to draw with crayons, only on certain walls in the house, which stopped the other problem.

"The first time he actually used the toilet like a big boy, everyone made such a fuss. His brothers and sister gave him hi-fives!!! That's all he needed. He's been using the toilet ever since."

Breaking things and courting danger. Like many children on the autism spectrum, Gabe did not have many inhibitions, which could be humorous but also stressful for the family. That was clear in a disastrous encounter with model airplanes when he was five.

"[Louis's brother] Michel had asked Louis to store his shiny model airplanes out of reach, just for a little while, in the basement. I brought Gabe downstairs with me to do the laundry, and after a while everything seemed too quiet. I found him in the room where Louis had put Michel's model aircraft."

Angélina can hardly contain a laugh, describing how Gabe was "playing" with the airplanes. "For Gabe, planes were supposed to fly. Needless to say, several of them were in very bad need of repair by the time he was done with them."

Angélina also recalls how Gabe managed to steal out of the house one morning at 4:30 and break all her fine chinaware. "He was not hard to put to bed, but now I had to lock the doors to prevent him from wandering at all times of the night."

Then there was the matter of the stove. Gabe loved to turn on the stove and pretend he was cooking. "One day," Angélina remembers, "he moved the chair to the stove to reach the knobs. I now had to watch him all the time." Angélina would remove the fuses from the stove every night before going to bed.

At the store. Grocery shopping with Gabe could be stressful, according to Angélina. “I couldn’t leave him at home and ask the kids to look after him. So we all went to Safeway together. Most times I would sit him in the shopping cart, but he also loved to walk in the aisles and look at everything. I had to follow him everywhere.”

Shopping brought along other adventures. One Saturday before Christmas, in the late seventies, Louis took the boys to the liquor store while Angélina prepared the *réveillon* (Christmas Eve dinner). When they came to the till to pay, Gabe stepped to the front, looked the cashier in the eye, and said: “Hold up!”

“The man took the phone,” Angélina says, “and made to look like he was going to call the police. Louis, usually such a jovial and carefree man, didn’t think that was funny. The rest of the boys sure laughed.”

The end of bike riding. One day, Gabe tried riding a bicycle under the watchful eye of Mike and Rick. After a number of practice runs, Gabe seemed to be getting his balance and building confidence. The boys, meanwhile, were tiring of running behind and holding the seat to keep him from falling.

“Ok, Gabe. Hang on! We’re going to let you go,” to which Gabe did not respond.

“It didn’t end well,” recalls Rick. “He ran straight into a tree.” That was it for Gabe’s bicycle riding career. He would have to try something where both his feet were firmly on the ground.

Special play room. From Gabe’s scribbler: *At home my Mom and Dad made a special room for play, read, and colour. My Dad painted that room all white because I liked to take a crayon and make lines all around the room. And we used all the space to cut from magazines pictures of food, toys, people, nice trees, anything we liked. Mom would make our special glue: it was flour and water. Dad made us some stools to sit on and painted them different colours. Mine was red. He had to screw them to the floor so I could not throw them around. My favourite* *was our picnic lunch at noon when we put the tablecloth in the middle of the room and we all sat around and ate our sandwiches and carrots.*

In cahoots with siblings. Gabe got plenty of help from his siblings to find trouble, according to Angélina. "Louis and I had gone to the Niakwa Hotel for a beer and to play some shuffleboard, when the police came to find us. They told us to take our time and not to worry, the kids wouldn't move. They were sitting on the couch at home, waiting for Mom and Dad."

It had been a rainy day and Mrs. Paterson's yard had become a magnet for six rambunctious siblings bored of being inside, without supervision. The kids then proceeded to turn Mrs. Paterson's yard into a sliding mud bowl, getting covered and soaked in the process, and creating havoc for Mrs. Paterson. This free landscaping job created much consternation for the usually mild-mannered neighbour, who eventually called the police.

An officer arrived promptly, recognized the Langlois siblings, and took them home, where he ordered them to sit on the couch, and not move until their parents arrived. The children were more than happy to comply. "They didn't want to spend the night in jail," jokes Angélina today. But the scene was not funny when Mom and Dad got home. "The couch was covered in mud and six sheepish kids."

Shiny things. From Gabe's scribbler: *Apparently, I liked to get away and do foolish things like opening the water taps of my neighbours' houses. My Mom hot on my trail, right behind me, spotted the running taps and closed them one at a time until she finally reached me and laughed. She cocked her head, took me by the hand, and smiled. We walked home.*

There was this house not far from my home that they were fixing. They took all the windows [storm windows] and stacked them beside the garage. When I saw this through our living room window, I got away again and went right for the pile of windows. You see, I did not tell you how I loved to break glass. I threw them down on the grass and jumped on it. The mister there came running and told me to go home, but I was having fun. Oh, my Mom is here! She looked all over my feet, legs, and hands. The man told my Mom: "I cannot believe that he has no cuts at all. He sure is Jesus' little boy." I had jumped on these storm windows barefoot and shattered several of them without a single cut on my feet. No wonder my Mom was always saying, "Thank you, God!"

Disappearing act. In French-speaking families, the term *fugue* is often used to describe times when children wander from home. While many children do this at some point in their lives, some children with intellectual disabilities are chronic disappearers. Gabe was one of them, and his *fugues* occurred in each of his childhood homes on Burns Way, Chandos Avenue, and Hull Avenue.

"When Gabe finally learned to walk," Angélina says, "he really developed a liking for walking away." He would not run away from home, he would just go for long walks where nobody knew where he was.

One day Gabe was gone for almost thirty minutes before Angélina noticed. After rounding up Mike and Rick, and looking frantically everywhere for Gabe and calling his name, she eventually called the police. She prayed, as she did so often, to Saint Antoine de Padoue, the one she turned to when she needed to find things.

"We came by a field about six or seven blocks away from the apartment, and I had a strong feeling that he was there. 'Gabe! Gabe!' Mike would scream. 'Gabe! Gabe!' Rick would scream too. I remember looking at these two little boys, so intent on finding their brother, and feeling very proud of them, but at the same time very worried that something might have happened to Gabe."

Angélina walked toward a pile of rubble and empty boxes. There he was, hidden by the boxes, just sitting there staring in the void, his hands moving as they always did when he was nervous or concerned. "I had found my little Gabe. He got up and gave me a big hug but didn't say anything. I walked home with my three boys, holding hands, happy to be together again."

There would be more such disappearances. "He could be so fast!" she says. "One time he climbed the fence in our yard; another time he dug a hole under the fence, using toys, and ran away. Thankfully, we would always get him back." It was also a blessing that the St. Boniface police knew Gabe and knew how to find him."

Keeping the hospital staff busy. When Gabe was five years old, he woke up with a fever and stomach ache, and appeared agitated. Since he could not talk yet, Angélina could not tell exactly what was wrong, so she called the doctor. He told her it was likely a bad cold; she should give Gabe baby Aspirin and lots of liquid. Despite following the doctor's orders, his condition only worsened, and the doctor finally called them in for an examination. The diagnosis: acute appendicitis. Gabe was immediately operated on, and Angélina was told Gabe would need to spend two weeks in the hospital.

As Gabe recounted in his scribbler, however: "*After four days the doctor asked my mother if she could take me home. They even put me in a room by myself and took everything out except my big crib. The doctor said the nurses don't know how to handle me...I even found a way to get out of my crib and out of the hospital, walking around. An intern saw me with my hospital PJs and took me back in. I wondered what all the commotion was about. I had a good time! Ha!*"

The doctors showed Angélina how to drain the bad fluid and clean the incision with antibiotic gauze and tape each day, following Gabe's bath. After one week of Angélina's attentive care, the doctor approved the removal of the tube, and Gabe was good to go. "*Mom, you did a good job!*" Gabe wrote in his scribbler. "*It took about two weeks and everything was A-OK. That was some serious operation—I almost lost my life and nearly died.*"

The toll on Angélina's health

In 1967, when Gabe was four, Angélina spent two weeks in hospital with pneumonia—likely brought on, in part, by the mental and physical exhaustion that came with raising six children, including one with autism.

"I can't go because I have to take care of Gabe," she told Dr. Jacques. The doctor, however, knew of a solution and made the necessary arrangements. Before Easter, Louis drove Gabe to St. Amant Centre, a facility for disabled children, for a one-month stay while Angélina recovered in hospital, and later at home.

"Of course, my mischievous moments were not over," Gabe related in his scribbler. *"At night they had to put me in the big, big crib. I could not get out. But I found a way to climb on top of the crib and reach the ceiling, and started to take the tiles off the ceiling. The nuns were so surprised and could not believe it. They phoned my Mom to see how she was and said they were so anxious for Mom to come and get me before I demolished the building."*

Both before and after her hospitalization, Angélina would visit her friend, Sister Georgette Pantel at the Chanoinesses residence in Winnipeg. Sometimes Georgette would stop by when taking a walk to say her rosary. They had been close friends since Angélina's time as a nun at Notre-Dame-de-Lourdes (see First Break, page 64), and had kept in touch. Angélina would take the kids for a walk to see Sister Georgette, or she would slip out of the house when Louis was home, once the kids were in bed.

Angélina could always count on Georgette's wisdom, compassion, and understanding. They would talk at length about life and about the challenges of raising a family of six. Georgette knew about Gabe's disability and his unpredictable behaviour. She understood how difficult it was for Angélina to care for Gabe, while giving the same love and attention to the other siblings.

On a number of occasions, the two friends had discussed the need for a special class for Gabe, and the lack of resources to provide him the learning environment he needed. Angélina once suggested, lightly: "Georgette, you should start a special needs class."

"I'd love to do that," Sister Georgette replied.

CHAPTER 4

Pushed to the Limit

> I don't recall ever raising my voice to him. Anytime we would go through a rough patch, I would kiss him, hug him, and tell him, "Ça *va bien aller, garçon*. Everything will work out, son."
>
> —*Angélina Langlois*

"Fire! Fire! Firemen!"

Gabe's screams, accompanied by the strong smell of smoke woke Angélina one spring morning in 1969 at their house on Hull Avenue. She jumped from her bed and ran out of the bedroom. She could see smoke at the end of the hall, in the living room.

The rug was on fire! The curtains were on fire! The chair was on fire! Sitting on the floor, holding a box of matches, was six-year-old Gabe.

Angélina called the fire department, grabbed a blanket, and tried to smother the flames, yelling to wake her family. Louis arrived and took in the scene, speechless. Angélina knew the anger was boiling inside her husband. How many times had he warned her that something like this could happen?

Within minutes, they heard sirens outside. Five wide-eyed kids watched the firefighters rush through the door, armed with extinguishers and axes. They quickly ensured that the fire was out, took down the curtains, the rug, and the chair, and carried them to the front yard. One returned to gather information for his incident report.

"That was a close one," he said, shaking his head. Then he looked at the five pyjama-clad children staring at him, mouths hanging open.

Louis stood with them, holding the box of matches he had taken from Gabe's hand minutes earlier.

"Don't play with matches, okay?" was the only warning the fireman would give the kids as he tipped his hat and made his way out to the fire truck. Louis walked back to the kitchen, the acrid smell of smoke heavy in the air.

"All I remember," Mike says, "is Mom hugging Gabe and making him feel better." The other siblings surrounded their mother and brother in the kitchen, staring down the hall at the charred wall.

"I can't do this anymore"

Breakfast took a little longer that morning. The kids were late for school, and Louis was late for work.

On his way out the door, Louis turned and looked Angélina in the eye, his lips quivering. "Écoute-*moi bien Angèle*. Listen to me, Angélina. This is it! I can't do this anymore. We need to do something before someone gets hurt." He turned, walked out, and slammed the door.

Gabe looked up at his mom with big eyes. Angélina stroked his hair gently, staring at the emptiness of the door, where Louis had just stood. She gently brought Gabe to his bedroom, tucked him in bed, and locked the door.

At her wit's end, exhausted, Angélina sought refuge in a place that had never let her down: prayer. She lay down, closed her eyes, joined both hands, and prayed.

"I did as I taught my kids to do," explains Angélina. "I talked to Jesus just like I talked with my best friend. I asked him to help me be strong, to point the way."

She fell asleep. A dreamless, deep, comforting, and healing sleep. When she awoke, the sun was already high in the sky.

That evening, while Louis stayed home, Angélina took a walk and once again visited her friend, Sister Georgette, on Kitson Street. She related the day's events and explained, between sobs, how she felt that something had to change. "Georgette helped me immensely," Angélina says. "She understood. Somehow she knew exactly what I was going through. She listened and gave me courage."

On Gabe's next visit to Dr. Ferguson, Angélina recounted the fire incident. He told Angélina he thought she was doing too much; she could very well be headed for a health crisis of her own. After all, two years earlier she had indeed spent two weeks in hospital with pneumonia.

"You need rest, Mrs. Langlois. Why don't you allow me first to place Gabe at Montrose School, which would give you some time for yourself and for the other children? A chance for you to recharge your batteries."

Angélina agreed to have Gabe enrolled in special classes at Montrose School while the doctor made the necessary arrangements to have Gabe assessed by specialists from the Mental Health Services of Manitoba. Soon, neighbours saw Gabe each day after lunch, holding his mother's hand, waiting in front of their house for the bus to take him to Montrose school. They had no reason to suspect that dramatic changes were taking place.

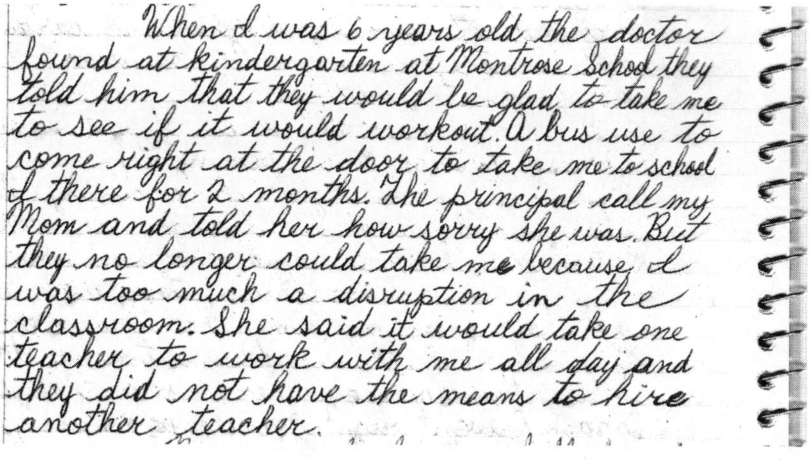
When I was 6 years old the doctor found at kindergarten at Montrose School they told him that they would be glad to take me to see if it would workout. A bus use to come right at the door to take me to school I there for 2 months. The principal call my Mom and told her how sorry she was. But they no longer could take me because I was too much a disruption in the classroom. She said it would take one teacher to work with me all day and they did not have the means to hire another teacher.

Gabe's scribbler entry about this episode

Angélina's health breaks down

Gabe's time at Montrose was short-lived, however, because Gabe's disruptive behaviour proved to be more than the staff could handle. And his mother's own health was once again becoming an issue. Just after Gabe's enrollment, Angélina thought she was suffering from hay fever or some other allergy. However, when she consulted Dr. Ferguson, he only pointed out the stress Gabe was causing her and how much time she needed to devote to him, while unconsciously leaving her other children to themselves.

"Doctor, I look after all my children. I know it's difficult but they are doing fine," she argued.

"Yes, but Madame Langlois, it's you who is not doing fine. You are in a precarious mental state and your body is showing signs of exhaustion. You must do something before you can't take care of any of your children." The doctor added that it wasn't only Gabe that would be affected; all of Angélina's other children would suffer if she were to experience a relapse and require hospitalization.

Dr. Ferguson now suggested it was time for her and Louis to consider placing Gabe in an institution for his own good, but also for the good of his entire family. Things had been getting worse and the risk of harm to himself or to his family was becoming very real.

The words of the doctor sliced through Angélina like a hot knife, bringing tears to her eyes. She knew that she and Louis would have to make a very difficult decision, very soon... Was she out of options?

Later that spring, Dr. Ferguson called Angélina into his office to discuss the evaluation report from the Mental Health Services specialists.

The very next day at the doctor's office, Angélina could feel her heart in her throat, the pounding almost too much to bear. She started to pray quietly as tears blurred her vision and rolled down her cheeks. She dabbed her eyes with a tissue.

"The specialists who assessed Gabriel strongly recommend his placement at the Manitoba School for Retardates in Portage la Prairie. Their concern is for Gabriel, but also for you and the welfare of the rest of your family."

"This can't be. I can take care of him," she assured Dr. Ferguson, sobbing. "I cannot abandon Gabe. That just isn't right."

"Madame Langlois, you know that if you absolutely want him at home, nobody can stop you. But I would ask that you and your husband consider the Portage la Prairie option most seriously. I am convinced it would be best for everyone in your family."

"That doesn't mean he would have to be there forever, right?" Angélina wondered. "I would want to visit him often, and when things are better, I will bring him home."

"I'm not sure of visitation arrangements, but I'm sure these could be discussed with the staff during the admission process."

The Mental Health Services evaluation was signed by Dr. Glen Lowther, Medical Superintendent at the Manitoba School for Retardates, a man who would influence the development of Manitoba's services to people with disabilities. Dr. Lowther wrote:

> The only favourable aspect of the report, is that the child is becoming more tolerable at Montrose School, which he began to attend recently for two hours each afternoon (Dr. Lowther had not heard of the last development with Montrose).
>
> He appears to be brain injured, although no medical evidence was obtained to confirm this. His present behaviour, however, indicates that the latter is a strong possibility. He has a short attention span, is easily teased and frustrated, and reacts violently to any interference with his activities.

Sometimes I would wake up in the night and see Mom at the dining room table, the light on. She was mending socks or sewing buttons—she would stop and say, "Come here, Gabriel." She would sit beside me, and give me a glass of milk. When I was finished she would take me back to my bed. She would cover me, give me a hug and a kiss, and say "Close those beautiful eyes and go to sleep, Gabriel."

—Gabe's scribbler

Dr. Glen Lowther

Lowther went on to list Gabe's destructive behaviours. "There is serious interference with family functioning... Mr. Langlois takes off in disgust, and describes Sunday (his usual day of rest) as 'worse than all six days at work put together.'"

Lowther noted that placement at the school had been suggested by the family's doctors a number of times over the past three years. Now, because of the havoc at home and in the community, he said, "it would appear that Gabriel's distraught mother should be relieved of her burden before she breaks down completely. We would therefore recommend immediate admission to the Manitoba School any Monday, as soon as this can be arranged."

There would be room for Gabe sometime in July.

After much soul searching and tears, Louis and Angélina decided to go along with the proposal; it was best for her and the rest of the family.

They would visit Gabe, and he could return home once his behaviour improved, they thought. This proved to be the most difficult decision for Angélina. She could not bear to say the name of the institution (in later years changed to Manitoba Developmental Centre); she did not consider her own son to be a "retardate."

BREAK

Angélina: Learning Empathy and Love

Men are what their mothers made them.
—*Ralph Waldo Emerson*

Angélina Langlois, eighty-four, has enough stories of Gabe to fill a book. But Gabe's stories are what they are because of his mom, and to understand Gabe's journey, we need to step back and look at the roots of Angélina's unwavering faith and fierce devotion to her son—and to her entire family.

Marie Virginie Angélina Dumas was born in 1931, in the village of Haywood, 80 kilometers west of Winnipeg. She was the eighth of twelve siblings: five boys and seven girls. Along with their parents, Daniel and Marie-Louise Dumas, they lived in a log cabin in the centre of the village.

Daniel Dumas worked hard to make ends meet. He would take on a number of jobs for local area farmers, including driving a combine and repairing farm equipment. Although money was tight, Angélina says, her family lacked for nothing: "The farmers who hired my Dad knew he had many mouths to feed, and paid him with fresh meat, poultry, eggs, and milk, in addition to a few dollars."

As in other francophone communities in Manitoba, the Catholic Church played a central role in Haywood. The Dumas family never missed Sunday mass. In fact, according to Angélina, no one dared miss mass in Haywood—even when it was held at four in the morning, in recognition of the farmers' need for uninterrupted days during the busy seasons. Father Jean-Marie Gagné led his flock with a firm hand.

Chosen and called

As a child, Angélina learned about the *Chanoinesses Régulières des Cinq Plaies du Sauveur* (Regular Canonesses of the Five Wounds of our Saviour), an order of nuns from Notre-Dame-de-Lourdes who ran the Dandurand School in Haywood. She knew the Chanoinesses to be disciplined and strict, yet also happy and fulfilled. For many girls, the young nuns represented strong role models. Devoting one's life to the service of God and others through the religious vocation provided opportunities for advanced studies, community, and friendships. From a young age, Angélina dreamed of becoming a nun.

In those days of large families, many families encouraged one or more siblings to join the clergy or a religious order. This helped the church fulfill its mission, to provide much needed ecumenical services, and at the same time lightened the financial burden of families.

One Sunday, only a few days after Angélina's twelfth birthday, the Dumas family hosted Father Jean-Marie for dinner. Following the meal, the priest stood, took Marie-Louise by the shoulders and announced that he had had a revelation earlier in the week: "I must tell you Madame Dumas, Angélina will go to the convent, I am certain of it!"

This pleased Marie-Louise, but not Daniel, who stormed out of the kitchen, fuming. Angélina was speechless. She knew she should be happy about this latest development, yet her heart was heavy at the thought of leaving her family, even if only to move to Notre-Dame-de-Lourdes, forty kilometres away. Her mother's teary eyes and her father's anger left her perplexed. What kind of birthday present was this?

Eventually the Dumas parents decided that Angélina would go to the convent. So it was that on a bright and warm August day in 1943, they watched Father Jean-Marie's car—he did have the biggest car in town—stop in front of the Dumas' house, in a cloud of dust.

Tears rolled down young Angélina's cheeks, which her mother dried promptly with her kerchief. "You will be fine, Angélina, you'll see," said her mother. "The Chanoinesses will take good care of you."

She ran to hug her father and felt as if he was never going to let her go. Today, Angélina realizes her father must have been thinking, "You're much too young to grow up this quickly."

The dust cloud from his car had long disappeared in the hot prairie breeze when Father Jean-Marie placed her suitcase in the trunk and opened the front door, inviting Angélina to sit in the passenger seat.

Angélina looked all around, taking in the sights, the sounds, and the smells of her Haywood home, the only place she had ever known. Reluctantly she took her place beside *Monsieur le Curé* and closed the door. She rolled down the window with difficulty and waved at her mom and dad, as the car rolled away from her home.

Father Jean-Marie assured her that she would enjoy the convent, that she would meet many girls her age, and make many new friends. She had heard many of his stories before and his sermons, and knew that several had not come true. Why should this one?

In the car, Angélina remained silent, feeling a mixture of anger and sadness over leaving her family. She was content to stare out the window as Father Jean-Marie whistled and sang.

"Would you like an ice cream cone, Angélina?" the priest offered. "We can stop at the store in St. Claude."

"*Tu peux bien la garder ta crème glacée. J'en veux pas*!" Angélina replied. "Keep your ice cream. I don't want it."

She had never been this far from home and Angélina noticed that the terrain was changing. It was very different from what she was used to, in and around Haywood. What looked like mountains or clouds lined the horizon on the left of the road, beyond St. Claude... very strange...

The terrain rose sharply after turning left at Rathwell and Angélina could see a number of small valleys where a multitude of streams flowed among the trees and the fields.

"These are the Pembina Hills Angélina," *Monsieur le Curé* explained. "Notre-Dame-de-Lourdes is on top of the hill, on the right. You will see, it is very pretty."

Indeed, it all looked very pretty and very new to her.

"Do you know the origin of the word Pembina, Angélina?"

After a few seconds of reflection, Angélina would impress *Monsieur le Curé*. Of course she knew.

"It is an Indian name for berries that grow across the mountain. It is good in jam or jelly."

"Very good! You have an excellent memory, my child."

As they approached Notre-Dame-de-Lourdes, however, the anticipation of getting to the convent gradually overcame the sadness of leaving home. They began to talk of the origins of the communities in the area: Lourdes, St. Leon, Bruxelles, Somerset, St. Lupicin, and Cardinal. Soon, Father Jean-Marie and Angélina drove up to the front steps of the convent. The sisters seemed very excited to see her.

The time for *Monsieur le Curé* to leave soon approaching, Angélina felt that she must say something nice to him, leave him with a good impression, to let him know she appreciated his thoughtfulness. After all, she liked Father Jean-Marie. She always enjoyed seeing the young priest on Sundays. He had a warm smile and bright blue eyes.

She walked toward him and offered her hand, which he took as he opened the car door, something he had done barely an hour earlier in Haywood.

"Thank you very much *Monsieur le Curé. C'est bien gentil ce que vous avez fait.* What you have done for me is very kind."

Life with the Chanoinesses

The Chanoinesses, as the nuns were officially known, first arrived in Notre-Dame-de-Lourdes on a fine summer day in June of 1895. Only thirteen days later, they opened their convent for classes, with an enrollment of forty young boys and girls. Forty-eight years later, Angélina Dumas entered very same convent.

The daily routine of Angélina and the other boarders seldom strayed from the established schedule: rising, individual prayer, school, breakfast, school, community prayer, dinner, recess, reading, bed. In her early days, Angélina found it all quite overwhelming. She cried many a night in the darkness of her room. She would bury her face in her pillow and sob, not wanting Mother Superior, Sister Marie-Céline, to hear her, lest she think doubts about religious life had crept into Angélina's young mind.

Angélina's solid bond with the Lord, however, grew from these teary episodes; she knew God had a plan for her life. "I talked to Jesus,

Angélina driving the sleigh

just as if he was right there with me. It was the only way I could survive," explains Angélina.

The Chanoinesses community offered many opportunities for young women to develop new skills. Although education and nursing occupied a prominent place, the operation of the convent allowed the nuns to perform a variety of jobs, including some that were normally considered exclusive to men. It was not uncommon to see a Chanoinesse operating the plough (or the sleigh in winter) behind a team of horses, pruning orchard trees, spinning or weaving cotton or wool, binding books, or planing boards for a bench. For a brief stint, Angélina even found herself managing the kitchen in Lebret, Saskatchewan, at the Scholasticate of the Oblates, feeding more than 500 seminarists—young men studying to become priests.

While the Second World War raged overseas and young men from neighbouring communities enlisted to fight, the calling of religious life became stronger and more constant for Angélina. During the summer of her fifteenth birthday, Angélina spoke with her mother and Father Jean-Marie about the possibility of becoming a Chanoinesse. Both could not have been prouder, and Father Jean-Marie agreed to recommend her as a novice.

On her return to the convent, therefore, she wrote to Mother Marie-Céline: "Reverend Mother, I come to respectfully ask you to admit me toward the taking of the religious habit." She explained that her need to serve others was strong. The feeling of accomplishment and the assurance she was spreading joy were sufficient reward for her. As her experience in the convent had taught her, the rigour and discipline of a nun's life did not mean that one could not enjoy life.

After several months of waiting, Angélina began her postulate (her probationary period) on February 2, 1946. Her first performance report, written by the director of novices, Sister Gertrude-Marie provides a colourful portrait of the young novice:

> Mlle Angélina was a fervent apostle in the crusade however was not gifted for studies. She enjoys manual tasks and applies herself in a manner consistent with her young age. Her health is fair. She is pious and quite attached to her vocation. She has a good temper, a little soft. Her judgment still requires development, however with time and solid training we believe she is capable of becoming a religious.

That August, at the age of sixteen, Angélina officially became Sister Denis-du-Christ-Roi, a name she chose as a tribute to Saint-Denis, whose headless statue adorned the front of the Haywood church. A two-year noviciate followed, symbolized by Angélina's taking of the nun's habit. In November 1948, Sister Denis successfully completed the exams required for admission to the profession. Finally, she would make her temporary vows, which would be in effect for up to five years before her permanent profession of a lifetime engagement as a nun.

Angélina, like most of her peers, showed a mix of pious devotion to her calling and normal adolescent energy. As the director of novices, Sister Gertrude, reported:

> In the beginning, Sr. Denis was flighty, eagerly seeking pleasure and enjoyment. She sought compliments, obeyed with ill temper, and ordered others without charity. In a word, she had all the faults of a spoiled child. During her noviciate she worked hard to correct herself. With sound judgment, and a rightful spirit, she

understood without difficulty the teachings of the noviciate. She is pious, happy, and skillful at work. Her will remains weak and she is easily influenced by her surroundings. It is therefore important to place her in a good environment to develop her personality and complete her training.

Convent Chronicles

The Convent Chronicles, a daily diary penned by one of the Chanoinesses, opens a window on daily activities and special events that Angélina experienced. The descriptive, youthful, and often poetic nature of the diary brings us back to a much simpler time. These excerpts help us follow Angélina on her religious journey and provide interesting peeks at her life as a Chanoinesse:

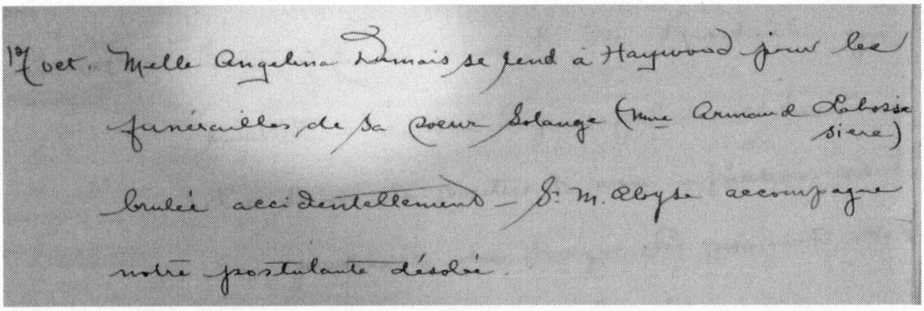
17 oct. Melle Angelina Dumais se rend à Haywood pour les funérailles de sa soeur Solange (Mme Armand Labossière) brulée accidentellement — S. M. Aloyse accompagne notre postulante désolée.

Excerpt from the Convent Chronicles

Death of Angélina's sister. "Oct 17. Miss Angélina Dumais [sic] goes to Haywood for the funeral of her sister Solange (Mme Armand Labossière), who died accidentally in a fire. Sr. M. Aloyse accompanies our sad postulant."

First snowfall. "Oct. 28. A beautiful white snowy blanket covers the ground and the evergreens display their cottony duvet... Will the snow stay? Will it go?... We bet on it... Peanuts to the winners!"

Grand Benedicamus. "May 1948. His Excellency, Mgr. Cabana visited us on the eve of Ascension Day to celebrate mass at the convent. Mother Superior decreed a day of rest and a Grand Benedicamus in his honour. [...] Our Chanoinesses' hearts rejoice on this beautiful feast of Pentecost, with its *matines* (morning bells). Grand Benedicamus!"[7]

Celebrations. On the occasion of Ste. Catherine's Feast—commonly known as "Old Maids" day—every November 25, the sisters would honour their young boarders with handcrafted presents, games, and prizes. Everyone enjoyed the Ste. Catherine's Feast annual toffee pull, as has been the custom in many French-Canadian families for generations, to honour St. Catherine, the patron saint of unmarried women. St. Catherine's day is sometimes known in Quebec as "toffee day," a day when marriage-age girls would make toffee for eligible boys.

Sacrifice

Angélina wanted very much to please Jesus by making sacrifices, a concept central to religious life, but in the early days, she was a little naïve as to what that meant. Working in the carpentry shop with Sister Marie-Elizabeth, Angélina noticed a jar of thumbtacks. Thinking these might help her get closer to the Lord, she slipped *une dizaine* (about ten) in her pocket for future use. The next day, she carefully stuck the thumbtacks through the bottom of her shoes, the pointy ends protruding inside. Five for each shoe, in keeping with the order's name Chanoinesses of the Cinq Plaies (five wounds). "It would be very little pain compared to what Jesus had to suffer, and a good sign of my sacrifice for him," thought Angélina.

The pain must have been excruciating; effectively Angélina was walking on thumbtacks, which eventually jabbed themselves into her feet all day. And to think that she would tolerate the pain, without flinching, first for five days, but then for four more "*pour une neuvaine*" (a novena, a period of nine days). Thankfully, her secret sacrifice would be uncovered in the laundry. The sister assigned to laundry

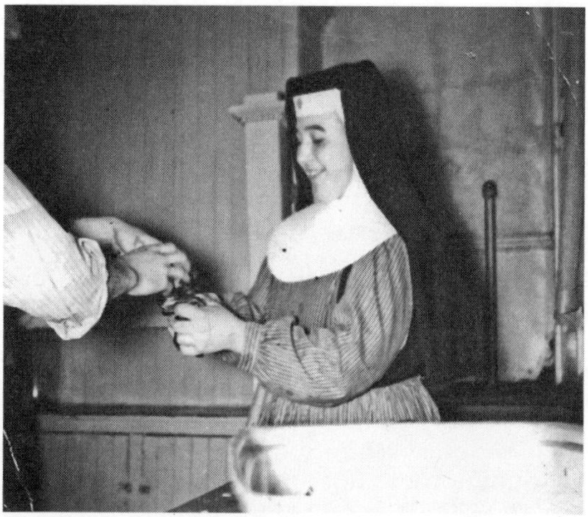

Angélina pulling St. Catherine's toffee

duties noticed the blood that stained Sister Denis' white stockings. She brought her discovery to the attention of Mother Superior, Sister Marie-Céline, who immediately summoned Angélina to the laundry room.

Sister Marie-Céline invited Angélina to follow her to a quiet corner. "Sister Denis, Sister Marie-Julienne tells me that she found blood stains on your stockings. Can you explain the significance of this?

"*C'est un secret Mère Supérieure.* It's a secret, Mother Superior."

"You know Sister Denis, whatever secret you have, you can tell me and know that it will not leave the confines of these four walls."

"It is a secret between our Lord and me, Reverend Mother."

"Sister, you can share this secret with me," the Mother Superior said, softly.

Angélina nervously revealed that she understood the need to make sacrifices, thus sharing in the Lord's suffering—hence the thumbtacks in her shoes. "I am making a very small sacrifice, and feeling very little pain, compared to what Jesus had to suffer, Mother Superior."

This was not the first time Sister Marie-Céline had to explain the subtleties of personal sacrifice and abnegation to her young charges. It would not be the last.

Taking Angélina gently by the shoulder, she invited her to sit and remove her shoes. Bright crimson blotches covered the bottom of Angélina's white socks where the thumbtacks protruded. Sister Marie-Céline gently removed the socks as tears streamed down Angélina's cheeks, partly caused by the physical pain, but also the emotional pain of letting down her friend, Jesus.

"You know dear Sister Denis, you cannot injure yourself for the Lord. He does not ask this of you.

Angélina sobbed. Undeterred by Mother Superior's explanations, she would find other ways to make "real" sacrifices, as she thought she should.

But Mother Superior was not done. "Angélina, what you did is very dangerous to your own health. This type of wound could cause infection, if left untreated. And you know what infection is? Infection could spread to your feet and your legs and require amputation!"

Angélina's eyes grew wider at the mention of this last word. In her classes she had learned all about infections leading to the amputation of limbs. Surely that is not what her friend, Jesus, would have wanted.

"The Lord does not ask for this type of sacrifice and pain from you, dear Sister Denis. Now promptly go to the infirmary and have your feet taken care of. This will be our secret."

Return to secular life

Toward the end of her temporary vows, Angélina was faced with the decision of whether to make her permanent vows. "I wasn't a saint, you know," she confesses. "Although my faith was very strong, I enjoyed the same things other girls of my age enjoyed, laughing, having fun. I did not think I had the strength to live such promises for life."

The contrite look on Angélina's face soon vanishes, as she explains: "I remember once forgetting cookies in the oven. The smoke brought me out of my reverie. I ran to the oven and pulled out the cookie sheet with the burning biscuits on it and threw them out into the snow. I was devastated! Surely, spoiling or wasting good food had to be in contravention with my vow of poverty. I eagerly confessed this sin to Father Champagne at our next confession, to which he burst out laughing so loud that the echoes of his laughter reverberated throughout the chapel. I couldn't help myself: I laughed, too, heartily."

"My dear Sister Denis, this is quite an innocent mistake and nothing to be ashamed of. It is certainly not a sin against our Lord," explained Father Champagne. "Go and sin no more!"

Others in the chapel had noticed the laughter and now snickered at the sight of Sister Denis' contriteness. Half way to the chapel door, Angélina remembered that Father Champagne, in all his excitement, had forgotten to assign her a penance. She retreated back to the confessional and asked for it, causing Father Champagne to let out an even heartier laugh.

"My child, it would only be fitting for you to say three Hail Mary. Go now!" he said with a wink and another burst of laughter.

In the end, the thought of making vows that she knew she was likely to break proved to be too much for Angélina to bear. "I discussed my fears with several of my closest friends, sisters, and even with my mother. I prayed for long hours, seeking His guidance. I explained how I felt to Sister Marie-Céline, who understood. She said, 'If your

First visit at home with her sisters. (L-R) Flore, Lorraine, Angélina, Denise, Aline, Claudette

heart and your faith are pulling you in that direction, then it must be the right direction.'"

In February 1953, at the age of twenty-two, Sister Denis du Christ-Roi became Angélina Dumas once again. She was sad to leave close friends behind, feeling she had let them down. At the same time, her faith remained strong; she knew her Lord would accompany her along her journey.

Georgette Pantel (also known by her religious name, Sister Marie-Augustine) and Angélina had become good friends at the convent. "Angélina," Georgette said, "today you begin a new journey, yet I know that our journeys are forever linked."

Little did they both know at the time that Angélina's true calling would be to raise a family that would include a child with special needs. Little did they know that Georgette would play a key role in that child's life, several years later.

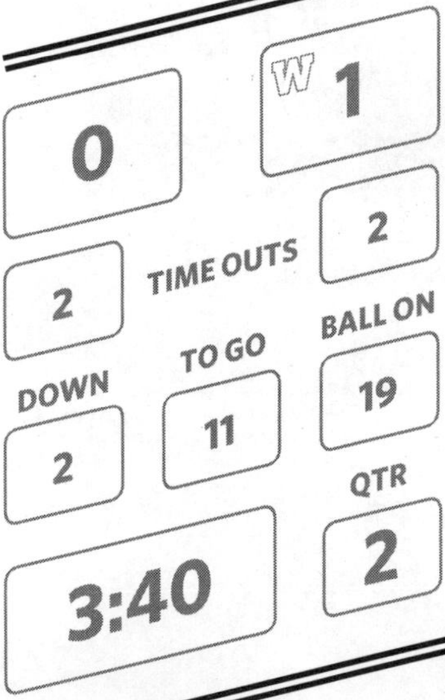

SECOND QUARTER

AWAY FROM HOME

HULL
14
50554#
Goldeyes
1

CHAPTER 5
Gabe Leaves Home

We must be willing to let go of the life we have planned, so as to have the life that is waiting for us.
—E. M. Forster

On June 12, 1969, an order was signed by Dr. J.L. Asselstine, Acting Director of Psychiatric Services for the Province of Manitoba. It declared that Gabriel Langlois was "a mental retardate within the meaning of the Mental Health Act" and ordered him to be confined as a patient at the Manitoba School for Retardates in Portage la Prairie.

That same day, he also wrote to Louis and Angélina informing them of the order. Gabe would be admitted on July 14, which coincided with Angélina's thirty-eighth birthday.

July 14 approached quickly. Angélina was sombre throughout the preceding week as thoughts raced through her mind. She busied herself making labels that read "Gabriel Langlois" and sewed them in the collar or the waistband of his clothes. She would often shut herself in her bedroom and cry in silence, while the kids played outside, unaware of the change looming on the horizon.

Saturday, July 12, was sunny and warm, but uncharacteristically humid for the middle of July, with a humidex of +40 C. Much to the kids' surprise, their father was still at home when they got to the breakfast table; he usually worked on Saturdays.

"*Ok, petits malins* (little rascals), get your bathing suits and towels. We're going to the beach." Louis did not have to repeat the instruction. The children downed their breakfast in a flash and were soon ready to go.

The Langlois family drove to Birds Hill Provincial Park, a forty-five-minute drive north of the city. They spent the day playing in the sand, running in and out of the water, thrashing about, screaming and laughing. The older boys switching from baseball to football to Frisbee, interrupted only by a mad refreshing scramble into the water. The younger kids splashed about, enjoying their fun in the sun. Angélina had prepared a picnic basket, and packed the blankets and everything else a family of eight needed to spend a day at the beach.

Little Gabe, however, spent little time playing with his siblings; he preferred to keep to himself. He made mud cakes and built a sand castle by the water's edge. He loved to destroy them, laughing as he turned them to rubble. His mother helped him to build them again.

"He loved water," Angélina remembers, "but I had to watch him closely."

That evening, the sun had barely set and not a sound could be heard in the Langlois household. The kids were all fast asleep, as if someone had sprinkled fairy dust. Angélina opened a beer for Louis and sat across the table from him. This had been a wonderful day, but Louis did not feel like talking. Finally, they went to bed.

Angélina stared out the window. A faint yellow glow was still visible on the western horizon and stars glittered overhead like diamonds on dark blue velvet. She awoke early, to the crack of thunder and the spatter of heavy raindrops against the bedroom windowpanes.

That day, after the clouds had cleared, Louis led the family on another excursion. "Écoutez-moi *bien, petits malins* (Listen good, little rascals)," he announced. "I am going for a ride and I think I will stop for '*un cornet de crème à glace*' (an ice cream cone). If you want one, better be in the car in five minutes."

But again, at the end of the day, when Louis and Angélina sat at the kitchen table, no words came to express the pain deep inside. Louis kissed his wife and went to bed, and Angélina sat for a few hours, her head in her hands, praying. Eventually, Angélina rose from her chair and took a few steps toward her bedroom. The sight of Gabe's suitcase, on the floor, stopped her. She stared at the suitcase for several minutes.

Gabe's things were packed "clean and in good condition", as the school had requested. The suitcase contained the clothes he would need for all seasons, shoes, and even Gabe's favourite toothpaste.

Monday, July 14, 1969

Six rambunctious kids got up excitedly, knowing that today was Mom's birthday. They were unaware that one chapter in their family story was being closed, and another opened.

For a third consecutive day, at Louis's invitation, the entire family got in the car. Dad was apparently not going to work today either. With the memory of Birds Hill on Saturday and yesterday's ice cream cone still fresh in their minds, the children could hardly sit still, even though the skies were grey and the pavement wet.

In the car, Angélina ensured that they had forgotten no one, and with a trembling voice, she turned to Louis and said, "*On peut y aller Louis.* Let's go." Had the kids taken a closer look, they would have seen tears rolling down their parents' cheeks, just like the raindrops streaking the windshield.

Louis drove north on St. Mary's Road, then headed west on Broadway and Portage Avenue. Soon they were out of the city, surrounded by endless farmers' fields, recognizing wheat here and barley there. Angélina and Louis said little until Mike asked, "Mom, where are we going?"

Angélina had dreaded the question. A complete silence fell on what had been a boisterous group only a second ago. Louis gazed straight ahead, a cigarette in his hand, his elbow leaning out the driver's window. Angélina turned and looked at Gabe who was staring out the window, unaware that he would not be returning home with his siblings that evening. Then she looked at the rest, who were staring at her, wide-eyed.

Angélina explained to the children that they had decided, on the recommendation of the doctor, to send Gabe to a special school where people would take good care of him. That it would be only for a little while, and that it was best for everyone.

Almost in unison, Gabe's siblings asked, "Why does he have to go away, Mom?" It was too much for Angélina to bear. She turned her head and sobbed.

Louis jumped in. "You know, Gabe needs special attention. People at that school will teach him and help him learn to talk and write. They will also teach him how to control his temper, and to behave properly."

Mike and Rick, at nine and eight respectively, were mature enough to understand the gravity of their father's words: this was a big deal. The others were bewildered at seeing their mother cry.

Gabe watched the vast fields of green, captivated by their swaying and shimmering in the gusts of wind, wave after wave.

A few hours later, the admission process completed, everyone hugged Gabe and walked back to the car. The Langlois family took the road back to Winnipeg, silent and uncertain of what would come next. One can only guess what six-year-old Gabe felt as he watched his parents and siblings drive away.

NOTES FROM THE ENTRY INTERVIEW

The decision to send Gabe to the Manitoba School for Retardates followed a series of consultations with Gabe and his parents, both in Winnipeg and at the school in Portage la Prairie. The following observations from the school records give an insight into life in the Langlois household that spring of 1969.

> **Father:** Steady worker—tries to be good to his children. Takes them out for Sunday drives and buys treats—but is very impatient with Gabriel. Has started going out more frequently at night in order to avoid the confusion at home.
>
> **Mother:** A quiet spoken pleasant lady who seemed to be able to restrain her emotions. Interview was constantly interrupted by Gabriel, who was in and out of the room several times; his absence was noted to be longer than usual and Mrs. Langlois either sent one of the other children to see where he was or she herself would leave to find him. She seemed to have excellent support with her other children who are always "looking out" for their brother.
>
> **Home and Home Conditions:** The home is in a good neighbourhood, but is poorly kept and in obvious need of many minor repairs. Not too clean and not too adequately furnished. The mother states much of this dilapidated state is due to the physical abuse administered by Gabriel (client).
>
> **Emotional:** Five siblings are all tolerant and considerate of their brother Gabriel. He, in turn, is quite the opposite. He does, however, show some consideration for his younger sister.
>
> **Habits:** Often wakeful—gets up and wanders away from home, naked—in the early hours of the morning.
>
> **Personality:** Likes to play with others, but only for short periods. He is easily teased and frustrated and reacts violently to any interference with his activities.

CIS
WESMEN

CHAPTER 6

Winds of Change in Mental Health Care

> Experts in the field were astounded by the results we achieved in Portage la Prairie at the time, results that many would have thought impossible.
>
> —*Anonymous*

Over the years, the Manitoba School for Retardates, now known as the Manitoba Developmental Centre (MDC), has been the subject of many papers, articles, discussions, and disputes.

In a 2013 *Winnipeg Free Press* article, Will Braun points out how, in its early years (its history dates to the late nineteenth century), the School was known for its lack of privacy, sometimes abusive staff, and neglect. Former residents speak of inhumane treatment, sometimes persisting into the 1960s and 70s, including the use of solitary confinement as a disciplinary measure. The buildings still have an institutional feel, with long halls, fluorescent lights, tile floors, locked doors, and, in some places, that sad antiseptic hospital smell. "Homey" is not a word that comes to mind.

Despite the pain of family separation, the timing of Gabe's admission to the School for Retardates turned out to be rather fortuitous. Winds of change had already started blowing a few years before his arrival. The treatment and care of people with mental illnesses and intellectual disabilities has continued to evolve since that time.

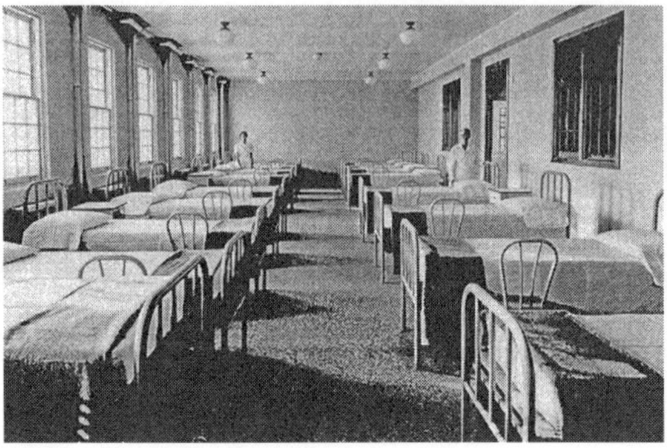

Glen Lowther, a forty-two year old psychiatrist from Scotland—he completed his psychiatric residency with the British Army—had been at the School since 1952. In 1965 he had assumed his Medical Superintendent role with a strong personal vision. As a consultant and board member with a number of other health organizations, his reputation as a mover and shaker in Manitoba's mental health services was well established by the time Gabe arrived.

Today, Glen Lowther is an affable, soft-spoken senior with a thick Scottish accent. He modestly avoids taking much credit for some of the groundbreaking changes that took place in Manitoba, in the area of services for people with mental retardation, under his watch. However, his leadership and conviction, combined with the willingness of his superiors and political masters to support Lowther's initiatives effectively set Manitoba on a trailblazing course. Lowther increased the school's staff complement and surrounded himself with strong people who could carry out the mission. He also formed a strong, mutually beneficial, alliance with the University of Manitoba's Department of Psychology, and its Dr. Gary Martin, Head of behavioral psychology.

Dr. Lowther had long been convinced that the quality of life of mildly and moderately retarded individuals could be enhanced greatly if they could live outside the institution, participating in programs with peers, and receiving services and care from qualified professionals.

In 2015, Jean Vanier won the Templeton Prize, in recognition for his tireless efforts and dedication to the cause of the most vulnerable people in our society. Information from L'Arche's website and a Templeton Prize press release provide Vanier's biography and the history of the organization he founded:

> Distressed by the plight of people with developmental disabilities, in 1964 he welcomed two men from an institution to live with him in a little home he called "L'Arche," after Noah's ark, in the French village of Trosly-Breuil. L'Arche grew quickly as this new way of sharing life together in community with people who would otherwise be shut away in institutions attracted many young people. And Vanier himself began traveling and speaking about his own life-changing experience of coming to know people with developmental disabilities.[8]
>
> Today, there are 147 L'Arche residential communities operating in 35 countries, and more than 1,500 Faith and Light support groups in 82 countries that similarly urge solidarity among people with and without disabilities.[9]

He wrote research papers presenting his theory and was called upon to speak on the subject at a number of conferences. One of these—the World Congress of Psychiatry—took place in Montpellier, France, in 1968.

Just four years earlier Vanier (whose vision shared some of Lowther's broad lines), son of Canadian Governor General Georges Vanier, had founded L'Arche, an innovative network of home-like residences for adults with intellectual disabilities.

Glen Lowther returned to Manitoba, armed with renewed energy and the belief that his goal, similar to Vanier's, could be achieved through initiatives like the Kin Glen Home in Portage la Prairie, with its striking similarities to the first L'Arche community in the French village of Trosly-Breuil, where the two men had met around 1966.

The Kin Glen Home

Kin Glen Home symbolizes some of the changes that were taking place in Portage la Prairie. Opening in October, 1966, as a pilot project, it was designed to demonstrate that retarded adolescents are more humanely cared for in home-like environment with peers than they are when they remain at home until an emergency requires admission to an institution.

According to a 1967 study, Dr. Lowther believed that the institution was equipped to understand the child and provide security, and that at a certain age a young person should live in family-like homes administered by the institution. The Manitoba School had developed strong recognition in the community, partly through public concerts by residents, and also through research and co-operation with the universities.

Dr. Lowther credits in part the Canada Assistance Plan (CAP) Act—established only three years before Gabe moved to the School—for the success of his reforms. The legislation provided funds that provinces could use to improve the quality and accessibility of provincial social programs. "All I had to do," Lowther remembers, "was convince my superiors that this was the right thing to do. Fortunately, they agreed."

In 1967, in an interview with Canadian Broadcasting Corporation reporter Warner Troyer, Dr. Lowther expressed his conviction that "communities, if they're given the opportunity, will take responsibility for their own moderately retarded and will allow them to live in their own communities, with their peers." Lowther pointed out that 400 people waited to enroll in the School while perhaps 300 residents did not need to be there. "The only reason they are here is because there is nowhere else to send them."

It was imperative, he said, to develop an "artificial alternative to the emotional support of the parental home. The essential place where a person grows is at home. For that moderately retarded adult to be constantly in the presence of people of an entirely different echelon of intelligence [in the institution] leaves them solitary, they kind of face what we call accompanied solitude."

Kin Glen Home became the test run for his vision, that every community would include a home for the moderately retarded—an ordinary house, large enough to be economically viable, with ten to fifteen residents.

Foster programs for the mildly-retarded

While Gabe did not live at the Kin Glen Home, he did benefit from a related initiative that Lowther began: the placement of residents in carefully selected foster homes. To be eligible for foster home placement, candidates had to be able to bathe, dress, and feed themselves. They would need to be able to attend school or sheltered workshops during the week, perform small household tasks, and care for their own rooms.

The young people accepted for foster home placements ranged from pre-school age to early twenties. It was assumed that the participating foster families were not in it for the money. In his comment on the program, René Toupin, then Minister of Health, noted that the families "have seen an area in which they can open a door of hope to an unfortunate fellow being, and the reward of watching the gradual improvement in their charges surmounts any monetary consideration."[10]

CHAPTER 7

Gabe's First Six Months at the Manitoba School for Retardates

I have discovered the value of psychology and psychiatry, that their teachings can undo knots in us and permit life to flow again and aid us in becoming more truly human.

—*Jean Vanier,* Becoming Human

As Medical Superintendent, Dr. Lowther does not recall any direct dealings with Gabe at the School. However, his daughter, Dale Brownlee, was Gabe's primary psychologist for the duration of his stay. Gabe's care would depend on a number of people, each with a role to play, including psychiatric nurses and attendants, consultants and possibly University of Manitoba interns responsible to deliver specific programs, medical staff (doctors, nurses, and aids), school staff, and social workers.

Dale's reports summarize the results of the evaluation panels—a team representing the various disciplines involved in Gabe's care—charged with reviewing residents' progress and making recommendations. Her reports allow us to follow Gabriel's progress during his stay at the Manitoba School. An entry in Gabriel's file six days after his admission, on July 20, documents the prescription of the drug Chlorpromazine, for a short duration, to observe behavioural patterns. Asked about Chlorpromazine, Dr. Lowther says, "Those types of drugs allowed the discharge of hundreds (probably thousands) of patients from mental hospitals into the community." The drug, introduced during the 1950s, had dramatically improved the prognosis of psychiatric patients worldwide.

Gabe's progress report from August 1969 provides details of his behaviour, condition, and diagnosis:

> **Personal History:** At the age of 3 years he was admitted to the Winnipeg Children's Hospital, for observation. It was reported on his discharge summary from hospital, on 24.1.66, 'As a child he never liked noise and would put his hands over his ears whenever he heard any noise.' He still does this and attempts to run into the next room. He also has a tendency to turn round in circles; he seems to enjoy this. In addition, he has very aggressive behaviour, running and climbing over everything. If he is thwarted he throws himself down on the floor and screams. The final diagnosis was autism.
>
> **Psychological State:** He rates as severely retarded.
>
> **Diagnosis:** Psychosis, possibly associated with some degree of retardation.
>
> **Prognosis:** He might be capable of simple training.

His next evaluation report a month later, seemed more encouraging:

> Gabriel presented as a somewhat obese child; taciturn and remote in manner. Most speech displayed (this was minimal) was in the form of mimicry of what was said by the examiner.
>
> The Wechsler Intelligence Scale[11] for Children was administered to Gabriel, to which little response was obtained. However, on subtest—Object Assembly—Gabriel scored at the near normal

level for his age, receiving a Scaled Score of 9, (normal or average being 10). This score may be seen as indicative of the boy's potential, providing that some of his handicaps can be overcome (chiefly autism, although some retardation may also exist).

On the basis of what responses were obtained from Gabriel to the WISC, an IQ of approximately 50 was estimated. However this cannot be seen as a particularly valid estimate, since only three subtests were scorably [sic] responded to. Gabriel was unable to count, to recognize colours or to use a pencil to any degree. Thus, reassessment should be done once the boy has received some training, with a view towards later placement in school classes.

Cottage Units at MB School for Retardates.
Courtesy Manitoba Archives.

Gabe resided in Pine Cottage, one of two cottages at the Manitoba School—two more cottages were added in 1971. These two-story cottages represented an innovative environment for residents and a radical departure from traditional institutional facilities and their large dormitories. For residents, it felt like moving from barracks to a home. The main floor housed the kitchen, recreation and program rooms, office, and a nursing station. A central staircase led upstairs to the cottage's sleeping quarters: rooms with two or three beds along with washrooms and showers.

Three months after his admission, Gabe showed sufficient progress to "begin school as soon as possible." The frequency of his reviews now moved to once every three months. His October report demonstrated steady progress and provided hope for the future.

> **Residence Report:** On admission, Gabriel was capable of doing a few things for himself. It appeared that everything had been done for him at home. He was unable to eat solids, but does this now, though he does not chew. Speaks only a few single words.
>
> **Training Report:** Gabriel has been participating in Pine Cottage's training program [Pine Cottage was the entry level cottage, for the younger residents who required more assistance]. He now uses a knife and fork, washes himself, and brushes his teeth quite well. He can dress himself with only a few prompts. Coordination appears good, as he can lace beads without any difficulty.
>
> **Recommendations:** Gabriel is to begin school as soon as possible, and to continue with training program in Pine. He will be reviewed in three months' time.
>
> Six months after his admission, things continued to look bright.
>
> **Residence Report:** Gabriel is doing well at Pine. He has learned to do many more things for himself, and now socializes a little better. Still speaks very little.
>
> **Recommendations:** Remain in school. Move to Lilac Cottage.

A subsequent note from his physical therapist attests to Gabe's further progress.

> This child was referred from the school with incoordination problems. I really can't see any incoordination at all. He plays ball well. He runs, walks, dresses, and undresses himself. He uses his hands for everything without any hesitation. He climbed up the bars and for the finer movements, he wrote his name quite well on a piece of paper, so I really don't think that he really has any problems that are big enough for us to do anything for him.

By the end of January of 1970, Gabe's progress was deemed sufficient to move him to Lilac Cottage. As Dale Brownlee reported, "He has learned to do many more things for himself, and now socializes a little better. Still speaks very little. Gabriel is attending school, but no reports are available as yet regarding progress there. He appears to be doing quite well, however. Recommended he remain in school."

Gabe liked Lilac Cottage, a newer building where he shared a room with only two other residents. He seemed to be adapting well to his new environment and showing progress on many fronts.

Well Christmas is just a few days away. My Mom and Dad are here to take me home for a two-week Christmas holidays. Christmas is so good, with all the gifts and games we play together and the good food: so much fun. Christmas has always been the best day of the year for me. My favourite holiday of all time....

I had a few days to get back in my routine. I am back in Portage. The Christmas holidays are over. But it is much easier now. I do all my work and then I have lots of time to look at comics; my favourite is Batman! And to watch T.V. before class.

—Gabe's scribbler

Photo of CP3120 by the CP Train Station in Portage la Prairie (2007) by Steve Boyko, traingeek.ca.

CHAPTER 8

Lost on the Railway Tracks

> Each time I heard the whistling train arriving at our station, I danced with joy. I just loved the voice of the train. Once my father said, "This boy of mine will not remain with us in the village."[12]
>
> —*Roch Carrier,* A Happy New Year's Day

On March 17, 1970, the Manitoba School staff noticed that Gabe was missing when the Lilac residents were assembled to go to a dance after dinner, and roll call was taken. After the grounds were searched, the school called the police and a search of the countryside followed. The details of how Gabe was lost are sketchy at best. Angélina remembers both Gabe and staff telling her of a field trip to the train station that day. Gabe's own recollection of that day's events is quite vague. The following reconstruction is based on what little we know about how it happened that Gabe was wandering along the tracks by himself later that evening...

Tuesday, March 17, 1970

Spring was in the air. There was a buzz at lunch on St. Patrick's Day, in the Lilac Cottage kitchen area. Serving and supervisory staff noticed that the residents of Lilac Cottage seemed louder and more excited than usual. The kids knew that the day's agenda contained two special events: a visit to the local train stations and an evening dance.

The beginning of March had dumped almost a foot of snow on the Manitoba School grounds. The younger residents had enjoyed rolling the sticky snow into snowballs and building snowmen. Hundreds of grassy pathways where the snow had been mysteriously removed criss-crossed the grounds, each leading to an alien-looking creature made of snow: some with scarves and toques, carrot noses and button eyes, and many with broad smiles.

That morning, many kids had screamed and laughed. Snowball fights had even broken out. But order was soon restored and those fortunate enough to have been involved in this snowy interlude were guided back indoors, red cheeks and runny noses.

Now, shortly after lunch, Gabe's group from Lilac Cottage boarded a bus for their field trip—an opportunity to cultivate social interactions among the residents and promote good relations with the citizens of Portage la Prairie.

Canada's two main rail lines part ways in Portage la Prairie, with the Canadian National heading northwest to Saskatoon and Edmonton, and the Canadian Pacific heading west to Regina and Calgary. In 1970, each line still had its own station in the town—the CN station on Fisher Avenue on the south side of the tracks, and a few hundred metres to the northeast, the CP station on Third Street Northeast. The Manitoba Pool and United Grain Growers grain elevators dominated the skylines nearby.

The constant movement of trains through the town—engines chugging, metal on metal screeching, shunting shock noises, bells, whistles, railway crossings lights flashing, bells ringing to warn pedestrians and motorists—all made for a true paradise for children of any age. Children admired the colourful and powerful locomotives. Such field trips provided a welcomed escape from the routine of the institution.

Gabe and his fellow residents first visited the Canadian Pacific station, where they met the station master, who explained the operations of the train station. The group moved from the ticket counter to the schedule board, running here, sitting there. Many had questions for the station master, but Gabe simply took it all in, quietly. The station master described how cars are shunted and moved to the elevators to be loaded with their grain cargo, or to the Campbell Soup's plant west of town to deliver cans to be filled with chicken noodle or tomato soup, and then pulled back and joined to other cars, to make a train that would deliver the cargo to its next destination.

The group then proceeded outside on the platform to look at the tracks, train cars, and equipment. A long freight train sat on the main line, its candy-striped locomotive's diesel engine purring like a big cat, steam billowing from its sides, its two bright lights pointing straight ahead. On the adjacent track, a smaller locomotive chugged by. Everyone jumped when the whistle blew loudly and the engineer waved from his window, a broad grin on his face, satisfied with the surprise he had caused.

Soon the time came to hop on the bus and drive across the tracks to the CN train station. After a very short ride, everyone filed out of the bus and assembled just outside the main entrance to the station, where they were met by another station master, dressed smartly in his uniform jacket and vest, with his brimmed hat and its golden band, and his pocket watch on a chain. He looked at his watch when the kids had finally assembled, returned it to his pocket and stared intently at the group in front of him. The entire group quieted immediately.

"Just in time," he said with a broad smile. "Welcome to Portage la Prairie's Canadian National Railway train station."

The group made its way through the passenger doors onto the elevated wooden platform. Outside, on the tracks, was a hive of activity. Locomotives moved about, switchmen threw switches then jumped on the moving train only to jump off once the switch was behind them, throwing it back and jumping on again to continue their ride. The kids were impressed at the men's agility; this was a dangerous job.

Gabe took in the entire scene at once, noticing the telephone poles, the tracks and cars, and the signals—some red, some green—on top of their tall posts. A sign in the form of an arrow caught his attention. He read the words aloud: "Winnipeg." That name he knew. Just as he had done during word association games with his mother, and later on at school, he thought of a number of words: family, home, and Mom.

A locomotive and a caboose sat on the nearest track, barely touching the platform, arranged especially for the group's visit. The staff split the group in two: one would follow the station master to the caboose; the other would accompany the engineer to the locomotive.

The wind blew harder, and Gabe shivered, as he joined the locomotive group. He covered his ears to shield them from the loud engine noise and to warm them at the same time. The sight and sound of the locomotive made his whole body tremble. The wheels were huge, bigger than any wheel he had ever seen. Smoke billowed from the four chimneys on top of the engine, just ahead of the windshield.

The engineer invited a few kids to follow him up the steps at the front and onto the walkway, which led to the locomotive's cab. Gabe followed timidly. After the locomotive tour, the group found the station master on the platform, ready to show them the caboose. "The caboose is used as the living quarters for the train's crew," he explained. "As you will see, it is almost like a small house on wheels. Please follow me, carefully, up the stairs."

Gabe and the rest of the group filed up the five steel steps and into the caboose, running their hands on the large brake wheel but unable to move it, thankfully. The look on their faces showed their amazement and the surprise; this looked like real luxury! The visitors made their way from the back to the front of the caboose, examining the coal-fired stove, sitting at the conductor's desk, checking out the bathroom and testing the plumpness of the pull-out bed.

Stepping out the front door of the caboose, the kids were again tempted to turn another large spoked wheel, without success. The school staff helped them down the stairs and herded them inside the station to warm up.

Gabe really had to go. He ran to the washroom door he had noticed earlier, found an empty stall and latched the door.

When he came out of the washroom, he looked around the station. The room seemed eerily empty. What had been a loud and busy place a few minutes ago was now almost deserted. Even the station master was nowhere to be seen. Had Gabe looked at the station clock, he would not have been able to tell that it was past five o'clock; he had been in the washroom for more than thirty minutes.

Gabe put on his toque and his gloves and made his way out the front door, looking for the bus. It was gone! He walked around the corner and made his way to the platform. The locomotive and caboose pair had vanished. Even the rail yard was quiet, except for the chirping of a few birds eagerly awaiting the arrival of spring. A deep fear quickly took a hold of him.

He looked up and saw that white arrow again, with the word "Winnipeg" in bold black letters. As he had done so many times before on Chandos Avenue, he followed his instincts and headed for home, and Mom. He turned back to Fisher Street and started walking east, following the direction of the arrow, towards Winnipeg. At Third Street, he turned north until he reached the rail crossing. Continuing north on Third Street would have eventually brought him to the Manitoba School, a familiar sight. Instead, he decided to follow the track.

Walking along the track and stopping frequently to look around, Gabe had a sense that things were not quite the way they should have been. He was seldom left alone at the Manitoba School, but here he was, by himself, on a train track.

The sun was quickly dipping toward the horizon; Gabe's shadow stretching further ahead of him on the railroad ties and the rocks in between. The wind blowing from his right chilled his face.

Something caught his eye in the snow-covered grass, a few metres from the track. He decided to explore. The sticky snow coated his boots as he made his way into the field. Gabe heard the railroad crossing bell chime and saw the big red eyes flashing. Then he saw the zebra-striped barrier swing down across the street to prevent cars from driving onto the path of the oncoming train. Waist-deep in grass and snow, Gabe first heard the train's whistle, then watched the train roll by with a comforting thumpety-thump, down the track.

Gabe returned to the track and continued his slow walk. He noticed that his shadow had disappeared. The horizon ahead showed hues of pink, purple, indigo, and grey, while the horizon behind offered a combination of red, orange, yellow, green, and blue. Soon, it would be dark.

The group from Lilac Cottage returned to the Manitoba School, ate dinner and readied themselves to go out for an evening dance. At 6:45 p.m., assembled, and ready to go, the staff checked attendance, and to their horror, realized that Gabe was missing. A frantic search of the rooms and the grounds produced nothing; nobody remembered seeing him at dinner. The staff promptly notified the RCMP that Gabe was missing. Much frenzy ensued.

Search efforts were deployed immediately on the grounds of the school and in the vicinity of the train station.

Meanwhile, back in Winnipeg, Angélina was playing bingo at the hall of Christ the King Church. She knew something was amiss when Mike came running into the hall. "Mom, you gotta come home, quick," he said, out of breath. "The police wants to see you!"

Angélina left everything on the table, grabbed her coat and left the hall right behind her son. The sight of the police cruiser in front of their house and two constables standing at her door sent a chill down her spine. The kids ran to meet her as she invited the constables in.

"*Bonsoir,* Madame Langlois. Have you seen Gabriel?" asked one of the constables.

"Why would I have seen him? Surely you must know that Gabe has been in Portage la Prairie since last July." said Angélina.

"We received a report from the Portage la Prairie RCMP that Gabriel is missing. I'm going to have to ask you to sit in the living room with your kids while we search your house. It's protocol, Madame Langlois. We just need to make sure he is not here. Sorry."

"I know he's not here! What happened? How is it that he is missing? Did he run away?"

The policeman understood her fears but could not alleviate them. "I'm sorry Madame Langlois, we didn't get any details. But we will let you know as soon as we hear more."

Angélina was frantic. She gathered the kids; they sat on the living room couch, quietly.

Once satisfied that Gabe was not in the house, the constable assured Angélina, "The RCMP is broadcasting the alert on the radio in Portage and in Winnipeg. They have search teams out looking for him."

"I cannot stay here and do nothing while Gabe is missing," Angélina said. "Who knows what happened to him?"

The officer advised Angélina to stay close to the phone. The police would call as soon as they received more details.

That just was not good enough. Angélina could not reach Louis who had gone out for the evening. She dialled her sister, Lorraine, explained the situation in a rushing stream of jumbled French and English words, and asked her if Ray (Lorraine's husband) could drive her to Portage la Prairie. Then she put the kids to bed.

"Mike, you are old enough to look after your brothers and Claudette. I know I can trust you. I have to go with Auntie Lorraine to Portage la Prairie because something happened to Gabe."

Mike nodded. "I'm sure everything will be fine, Mom. He's probably hiding in a closet," he said with a bit of humour. Angélina hugged Mike. Then she prayed once more to St. Antoine de Padoue, as she so often did when Gabe would wander from home. Her favourite saint, the one invoked for the recovery of lost people and things, had never let her down.

Angélina, nervously watching from the front window, saw Ray's car pull up. She was already out of the house by the time he beeped the horn. They made their way to Portage la Prairie as fast as they could. As they approached Portage, a strong premonition took hold of Angélina.

"Pull over Ray. I have a sense that Gabe is somewhere near here." Ray stopped the car on the shoulder, just beyond the intersection of the Trans-Canada Highway and Highway 26. Angélina stepped out of the car and walked toward the field. Somehow, she thought it felt much colder out here than it had in the city less than an hour ago. Minus 5 Celsius would be cold for any little boy lost out here and afraid, but it would be especially frigid and scary for her autistic son, missing for more than six hours.

Angélina noticed her shadow onto the snow and thought that the half-moon's light would be good for Gabe, wherever he was. The clear prairie sky was dotted with a million stars, more than Angélina had seen since her days in Notre-Dame-de-Lourdes, far from the city lights.

The trio got back in the car once Angélina was satisfied that there was nothing they could do out here. However, she was filled with a renewed optimism, hopeful that they would find Gabe tonight. They continued to the RCMP detachment, where the duty officer provided them with the latest progress update. Teams were searching the area around the train stations and the fields surrounding the Manitoba School. Alerts were being broadcast every ten minutes.

"Nothing leads us to believe that Gabriel might have been abducted," the constable reassured Angélina, her sister, and her brother-in-law.

After some anxious moments at the RCMP detachment, the constable in charge approached Angélina. The detachment clock's bell tolled twelve times.

"Mrs. Langlois, we're doing everything we can, and I'm hopeful we will find your son. I would suggest you get over to the Manitoba School. That's probably the best place to wait."

Angélina thanked the officer.

It was 12:15 am when they walked in to the Middlecourt building, the Manitoba School's hospital unit. Staff offered them coffee and instructed them to sit in the waiting room, but sitting was the last thing on Angélina's mind. An infirmary attendant, dressed in white medical garb, raced to Angélina after what seemed like a lifetime.

"We just received a call from the RCMP notifying us that Gabriel has been located," was all he said. "They're bringing him in by ambulance."

The hospital's clock showed one o'clock.

They brought Gabe in on a stretcher, wrapped in blankets. Angélina rushed to hold him; he felt really cold. His eyes were closed shut from all the crying he had done. He smiled warmly when he recognized his mother's voice. It seemed to Angélina it had been an eternity since she last hugged her son.

The medical staff busied themselves around Gabe. His pants were soiled and frozen. His lips were blue and his face showed signs of frostbite, with raw, white patches on his cheeks and nose.

Gabe screamed when the doctor removed his boots and socks and Angélina noticed that his toes were swollen and of a bluish colour. The nurses removed Gabe's cold and wet clothes and covered him with warm blankets, wrapping him into a comforting cocoon. Another nurse took his temperature, something they would do regularly over the next twenty-four hours.

The doctor asked Angélina to accompany him as he walked out of the examination room. They were met immediately by Lorraine and Ray, anxious to hear the prognosis.

"Mrs. Langlois, we'll take good care of Gabriel. Obviously he spent a long time out in the cold and we'll need to warm him up and keep an eye on him over the next couple of days to ensure there's no permanent damage."

The doctor's observation notes included, "No skin loss on face, upper extremities and torso. Feet cool surfaces, no loss, bluish at medial aspect." He later ordered a warm air treatment to raise Gabe's core temperature, ASA to make the tingling pain more tolerable as the extremities thawed out, and general nursing care. The RCMP constable walked over to Angélina, meaning to give her the account of the last eight hours, to the best of his knowledge.

"Mrs. Langlois, let's sit down. It's quite a story."

Angélina took a seat beside the constable as everyone else huddled over and listened eagerly.

"We believe that Gabriel was somehow inadvertently left behind at the CN train station, when the bus returned to the school at approximately 4:30 pm. From there, it appears that he walked along the tracks toward the eastern limits of town."

"Where did you find him?" A question that came from all directions.

"A gentleman was going home on the east side of town and slowed down as he approached the rail crossing. He thought he saw something move out on the tracks, in the distance, so he stopped and took a look."

"*Pas possible*," were the words out of Angélina's mouth, a barely audible whisper. "That's impossible." St. Antoine de Padoue had answered her prayers, once more.

The constable put his hat on. "Gabriel is a lucky boy," he said. "He was almost three miles away from the train station when he was found. I don't know if he would have made it through the night. I'm very happy for him and for you." He looked forward to writing up that incident report.

"My Mom was pretty nervous. She was there for thirty minutes and wanted to go look for me, but the police said it would be better for her to stay there because they were contact with the police and the volunteers looking for me. It was just about 10:00 p.m.[13]*, when the police received a phone call from the hospital. They said some gentleman brought a boy in, that he had found him on the railroad track in Little Portage (that is just [east] before Portage la Prairie).*

"The doctor told my Mom that I was very, very cold and a little frostbite on my cheek, fingers and toes. I've been frost bitten a little. I could have been hypothermia. I almost froze to death. But it was not severe. They would keep me in the hospital for a few days to make sure that I would be all right. My Mom stayed with me until I feel [sic] asleep. That was another close call for me. I thank God for saving me."

—Gabe's scribbler

After he had fallen asleep, Angélina kissed Gabe good night and joined her sister and her husband for the ride back to Winnipeg. Louis and the kids would not believe this story... *Spring arrives on Friday,* Angélina thought; *it will be a glorious day.*

The identity of the Good Samaritan who ventured out of his way on that cold Saint Patrick's night was never revealed to Angélina. To this day, this person has remained anonymous. This is a fitting opportunity for Gabe, Angélina and the rest of the Langlois family (and all of us, Dancing Gabe fans) to express their gratitude and their sincere appreciation to you, whoever you are and wherever you may be.

KENWOOD
91
W
MASRC

CHAPTER 9

Progress at School, Longing for Home

> Life consists not in holding good cards but in playing those you hold well.
>
> —*Josh Billings*

Back in Winnipeg, his siblings adapted to life without Gabe at home. Yet, they missed their brother. It was difficult for all the siblings to grasp the meaning of the situation. It was also difficult for a six-year-old boy to understand why he would only see his siblings on some weekends and at Christmas. And it was heart-wrenching for parents to explain it to them.

Louis settled into a less emotionally charged and stressful routine. Trying to make ends meet and getting involved in his other kids' lives outside of the home kept him occupied. As for Angélina, she never quite adjusted to not having Gabe around. Without Gabe to spice up the family's days, the winter days and nights seemed so long and cold.

> *It is now spring and the snow is all gone, thank God! I still remember that cold, cold snowy night when I got lost...*
>
> *Our yard is all dry so it's time to clean up. We have to rake all our yard and clean the flower beds. Our yard [Lilac Cottage] was the best one, so we got special treats and a movie downtown: Good times!*
>
> —Gabe's scribbler

Gabe recovered well from his railroad track escapade, none the worse for it. Gabe visited Middlecourt on a number of occasions that year, dealing with a number of minor physical ailments. Exactly a month after his rescue, he spent a week at Middlecourt, the School's medical building, with an upper respiratory infection. Later, in November, he returned to Middlecourt with severe tonsillitis, which meant two weeks in treatment.

However, on the intellectual side, Gabe continued his steady progress. Already, in June, he showed remarkable skills in reading. He was given a special summer program to prepare him for school in the fall. According to the school's report:

> Gabriel was referred to the Evaluation Clinic on June 11, 1970. His health has been good since the last clinic. He fits well into Lilac Cottage, getting along well with both staff and other residents. Gabriel loves affection and cuddling.
>
> **School.** Gabriel still appears mildly autistic. He socializes little; can play with only one other person at a time. Behaviour and attention span are good. Gabriel seems interested in all school activities. Academically, Gabriel knows his colours, counts well up to at least 20, and answers most questions in class. He can read at an advanced level for his age (Grade III words). On the Metropolitan Readiness Test,[14] Gabriel obtained a score of C, with his highest scores being in the areas of word meaning, matching, and alphabet.
>
> Gabriel is to be given a special summer program, hopefully by a member of the teaching staff, first on an individual then a group basis to develop his abilities. He should thus be ready for educable work next fall. To be referred for a hearing test.

"He was growing up, learning, and developing confidence," explains Glen Lowther. Connecting the dots of each consecutive report, the clouds on the horizon begin to dissipate, slowly, and rays of hope begin to shine.

The school's assessment was also encouraging:

Psychological Report: Gabriel has been a resident here for approximately one and a half years, and has shown constant progress since his admission. Gabriel presented as a still remote, but decidedly improved young boy. He still would seldom reply directly to questions, but rather would mimic what had been said to him. He was extremely fond of pencil work of any type and both printed and read a good variety of words.

Visual motor co-ordination was good (at 5 1/2 year level) as was arithmetical reasoning. On the other hand, as might be expected from Gabriel's autistic manner, verbal fluency, and general comprehension (judged by answering various questions) were considerably lower.

Residence Report: Gabriel's personal hygiene is good, but at times he must be reminded to wash his hands after using the toilet. His table manners are very good. Gabriel communicates quite well, and will occasionally start conversations with staff and residents. He plays very well with the other children and likes attention. His temper control is good, but at times he can get quite upset if things don't go his way. Gabriel has shown some improvement since coming to Lilac Cottage.

Training Report: Gabriel attends a primary educable class with Mrs. Trimm. In school his progress has been very good, and he has been reading for some time now.

Recommendations: Gabriel will remain at Lilac Cottage and at school. Gabriel has made good progress since his arrival at the Manitoba School. Reassessment will be carried out in a year's time to measure further advancement. (Signed by Dale Brownlee)

Angélina, too, was encouraged by his development. "I had noticed changes in Gabe with every successive visit," she says, proudly. How much progress could he make? How far could he go?

DANCING GABE
91
ORLANDO

CHAPTER 10

A New Place, a New Family

When one door closes another door opens. But we so often look so long and so regretfully upon the closed door, that we do not see the ones which open for us.

—*Alexander Graham Bell*

On Sunday, September 26, 1971, Premier Ed Schreyer traveled to Portage la Prairie to deliver a speech to parents, friends and citizens assembled for the sixth annual Open House at the Manitoba School for Retardates.

Dr. Glen Lowther met the premier at his office in the Administration Building and accompanied him to the Team Room where the visitors were assembled.

The Open House, with its guided tours of the units and training programs, its sale of handicrafts made by the auxiliary, and its fund-raising raffles always attracted many people from the neighbouring communities. It brought new faces to brighten the residents' day, along with casual conversation, a little affection, and snacks.

One interested guest who came to hear Premier Schreyer's speech that day was Edith Boissy (not her real name)[15]. She had come to the Open House for the previous three years. The announcement from her local paper had been posted on her church bulletin:

> **Retardates School Sets Open House**
> The staff and auxiliary of the Manitoba school for retardates will hold the sixth annual Open House and tea 2 to 4 p.m. Sept. 26 at the school, Third Street NE, Portage la Prairie. The auxiliary will sponsor a sale of handicrafts and home baking.
>
> Guided tours of all units will take place 1:30 to 4 p.m. when training programs will be in progress and work done by residents on display and for sale. Two new cottages will be officially opened during the day.
>
> Premier Ed Schreyer is expected to attend.

Edith had invited a girlfriend to make the seventy-five-minute trip with her and her children from Treherne to the Manitoba School. It was a chance to bring some joy to others. When you give joy, invariably you get some back, she knew.

She and her friend had signed the guest register. She had then led her small group through the crowd and helped them get juice and cookies, mingling with the residents and other assembled guests. She had saluted some acquaintances while taking in the somewhat chaotic scene.

Now the room quieted instantly, the loud chatter suddenly replaced by an almost church-like silence, when a gentleman tapped the microphone and introduced Premier Ed Schreyer. The Premier proceeded to the podium and addressed the crowd.

> Today I am addressing an unusual group of people—a group that shares a heavy responsibility, great frustration, I should think, and simultaneously hope.
>
> It is not for me to tell the parents, and the staff, here, and all associated with the auxiliary, just what that burden of responsibility entails, despite the love and affection that is ever-present, nor indeed the hope that we all must cling to....
>
> I do note that you have been successful in influencing public awareness concerning retardation. It is most encouraging to note the change in public attitude toward the care and treatment of

> those so afflicted. This is so because all involved with the families and professionals working in this field have brought some public attention. This is the age of blunt fact and open acknowledgment of problems. Long past, we may be thankful, is the day when retarded members of the family were hidden away in pretended non-existence and never mentioned. New concepts in treatment and training have made it possible for such persons to receive care, to be trained to their utmost capabilities, and to become, in some cases, able to function quite well in society.

Premier Schreyer provided four encouraging examples of rehabilitation. First, increases in education, vocational training, and rehabilitation services allowed the "lesser retarded" to contribute to their community. Second, more than 150 former "moderately retarded" residents now lived in community residences and foster homes, following the model established by the Kin Glen Home in 1967. Third, the "multiply-handicapped" would soon benefit from new facilities incorporating advanced concepts, design, and equipment to provide improved environments for their development. Finally, a pilot program to place the "severely and profoundly retarded" into the Portage la Prairie community was nearing launch, after they had been trained in self-care, social interaction, and domestic work.

Premier Schreyer continued:

> Thus we have come a long way since the time the school was established back in the 1880s as a Home for Incurables, and since the period when custodial care was all that could be provided for those unable to make out in the everyday world.
>
> The retarded child can be present in any family, and mental illness or various forms of psychosis can afflict any one of us. The pressures and tensions of the modern world contribute greatly toward the increasing number of men, women, and yes, children too, who find it difficult to cope with mounting problems.[16]

A lot of energy packed in a small container, Edith Boissy enjoyed interacting with the residents, especially the little ones. She was a hard-working farm woman, all of five-foot nothing, with a head of curly hair framing sharp brown eyes, and a devilish smile attesting to her love of laughter. She made children laugh, and they made her laugh. Edith joined the crowd that toured Lilac Cottage, where she met a number of the young residents, including Gabe, proud to show-off their clean rooms. The kids greeted their visitors enthusiastically and ushered them through the facility.

The day slipped away, quickly. The visitors were soon on their way home, their minds filled with a jumble of memories and thoughts, satisfied that they had brought happiness to a number of residents, and received happiness in return.

That spring, the visit to the Manitoba School was already a long-forgotten memory when the ringing of the phone brought Edith Boissy out of her reverie.

"Hello," she answered, unaware that the call would change her life, and someone else's.

"Mrs. Boissy, this is the Manitoba School for Retardates calling." She did not recognize the voice.

"Yes... How may I help you?" she replied.

After introducing herself, the person at the other end explained the reason for her call.

"Mrs. Boissy, you visited the School last September during the Open House, and it seems that one of our residents had taken quite a shine to you. You had also expressed an interest in fostering a resident, given the right opportunity."

"Yes, I remember one particular little boy being quite affectionate. He followed us around most of the afternoon. He was very cute."

"Yes Mrs. Boissy, his name is Gabriel. He is now nine. He has made amazing progress while at the School and the staff feel he would benefit greatly from living in a normal family setting, possibly with other children, and going to a normal school."

"What's wrong with him?" asked Edith.

"I wouldn't say that something is wrong with him. He is just a little different than what most of us are used to. Gabriel has mild autism, which causes some behaviour issues, but he has learned to control these and he's been doing very well in school, and getting along fine with others."

"I will have to discuss this with my husband and get back to you," answered Edith, bringing the conversation to a close.

The person at the other end of the line had been referring to a recent evaluation report on Gabe, signed by Dale Brownlee on January 11, 1972:

> **Psychological Report:** Gabriel was reassessed on the Wechsler Intelligence Scale for Children, scoring as follows: Verbal IQ—70, Performance IQ—86, Full Scale IQ—75. These scores show tremendous progress since admission. Gabriel has previously scored IQs ranging from the low 50s at admission to 64 last year on the Stanford-Binet.
>
> **Residence Report:** Gabriel looks after his personal hygiene very well. He has a little difficulty making a bed. Gabriel communicates well with other staff and residents. Because he is a bit of a sissy, other residents pick on him at times, causing him to become very upset. Gabriel is very good at reading and writing, and spends most of his spare time on the ward doing so.
>
> **Training Report:** Gabriel attends Mrs. Trimm's class for educable children full days and is progressing extremely well. In Arithmetic, he is working at the Grade 3 level, while in Phonics and Reading, at the Grade 2 level. Gabriel has some difficulty responding to spoken instructions, however when they are written down for him, he generally succeeds. In the same token, Gabriel often can write what he wants to express better than he can verbalize it.

> **Recreation Report:** Gabriel participates fairly well when motivated. He likes bowling, although he lacks in coordination. He socializes well with residents and staff. His coordination is poor.
>
> **Recommendations:** In view of his tremendous progress over the past year, it was felt that Gabriel is ready for foster placement, as well as inclusion in a regular Grade 2 class. [Our social department staff] will be speaking to Mr. and Mrs. Langlois about these possibilities. In the meantime, School Division #24 will be approached regarding placing Gabriel in a downtown school class.

Mrs. Brownlee's recommendations triggered a number of events in a very short time frame. Circumstances being what they were, it is doubtful that Gabe ever had time to attend a downtown class in Portage la Prairie.

Gabe, now nine years old, was unaware that he had reached this important crossroads. His next steps were decided for him and recorded in a legal document, signed by the Director of Psychiatric Services on the 13th day of March 1972:

> In the matter of The Mental Health Act and in the matter of Gabriel Joseph Langlois, a mental retardate.
>
> Whereas on the 14th day of July 1969, I did order that Gabriel Joseph Langlois be placed as a patient in the Manitoba School for Retardates, and whereas it now appears to me to be in the best interest of the said Gabriel Joseph Langlois, and of the public, to vary that order,
>
> I HEREBY ORDER that the said Gabriel Joseph Langlois be allowed temporary leave from the above, and placed on probation under the supervision of the said Mrs. Boissy (friend) of Treherne, Manitoba, for a period of six months from the date of this order.

Moving to Treherne

Monday, March 13, 1972

Gabe laid his head on his pillow and closed his eyes. He couldn't help feeling excited, although not quite certain why. Nurses had helped him pack his suitcase that afternoon and told him he was going to live with a nice family, on a farm.

The next morning, Gabe performed the same routine he had followed for three years—brushing his teeth, combing his hair, and making his bed, always in the same order. When he returned to his room after breakfast, Bill Milburn, his psychiatric nurse, was waiting for him, along with other staff, dressed in their white uniforms. Gabe also recognized Dale Brownlee, smiling gently at him.

His suitcase sat on his bed, the bed he had made so carefully before breakfast. Gabe could feel that something special was happening, but he could not say what. He had never seen a crowd in his room. Had he done something wrong?

"Gabriel, we're going to miss you," said Dale. "You have made such progress that it's time for you to go and live with a family, and go to a normal school."

Not really grasping thes significance of her statement, Gabe said nothing.

Bill picked up Gabe's suitcase while the rest of the staff took turns hugging Gabe and saying their goodbyes, misty-eyed. He liked hugs but he was confused at seeing them sad.

"Let's go, young man!" instructed Bill. "We have an important rendezvous," he said, as he took Gabe's hand and led the way out of Lilac Cottage.

Gabe followed Bill, looking behind him at the assembled group, waving his free hand frantically as they waved back.

"Bye! Bye!" he yelled, trying to keep up with Bill.

"Goodbye, Gabriel," they replied, in unison.

He jumped into the passenger seat. He watched attentively as they drove away from Lilac Cottage, the only place he knew as his home for the past two years, unaware that he would never return. Out to his right, he recognized the building where he ate his meals. The sun was shining bright, warming his face through the car window, and Gabe noticed buds sprouting on tree branches. Snow was melting, announcing new beginnings.

Gabe took one last look at the Manitoba School for Retardates. Soon houses gave way to snow-covered fields. They had been out of town for a few minutes when Bill pointed to a low-flying yellow airplane to Gabe, on approach to the airport.

"Look Gabriel, he's landing," explained Bill.

Gabe read out loud to Bill the words he could read on a large sign by the side of the road.

"C.F.B. Portage la Prairie."

"That's right," exclaimed Bill, with a broad smile. "Do you remember visiting the (Canadian Forces) base and seeing the airplanes?"

Gabe nodded, as he read once more, the words on another sign on the fence topped with barbed wire.

"Department of National Defence. No trespassing," he said.

Gabe read the names of the towns they passed: "St. Claude, Rathwell." Unaware, he was following the same road his mother had taken to the convent in Notre-Dame-de-Lourdes almost thirty years before, in the company of Father Gagné (see "First Break," page 61). Like her, he was mesmerized by the hills rising on the horizon.

Bill slowed the car and turned left toward the hills. Gabe read the sign as they drove by: "Treherne."

The pavement soon gave way to a muddy road up through rolling hills sprinkled with patches of forest, among farmers' fields, the sun melting the snow under a cloudless Manitoba sky. A few kilometers further, they turned into a small drive through a thick border of tall trees, and emerged into a farmyard. A small dog ran toward the car, barking loudly, but Gabe just smiled at it.

As Bill brought the car to a stop, Gabe gazed at the scenery, which looked just like pictures of farms he had seen in his school books—the white two-storey clapboard house on his left, the white picket fence ahead, the gate at the end of the gravel drive and a yellow school bus, cattle grazing within reach of the fence, a silver grain bin, outbuildings, a barn straight ahead, and a garage. Beyond the buildings Gabe could see a small pond and rolling fields stretch out to the horizon.

A few moments later a woman with curly hair and bright brown eyes walked out of the house and quickly closed the distance to the passenger door, a broad smile lighting her face. A face Gabe knew he had seen before.

He opened the passenger door and stepped out, his boots sinking in the mix of mud and snow, the smells and sounds of the farm flooding his senses: the smell of the wet hay, the mooing of the cows grazing in the meadow, the clucking of the chickens in their coop barely fifty feet away, and the barking of that little friendly dog.

Edith waited for him to close the car door and met him in a warm embrace, which took Gabe by surprise. He watched a man open the fence gate and walk toward them, his tall rubber boots muddied, his checker-patterned wool jacket open, holding his gloves in his bare hands, a cap on his head. He too smiled at Gabe and offered his outstretched hand, which Gabe shook timidly after a long moment of hesitation.

"Hello Gabriel, welcome to our home," Edith said in a friendly tone, while her husband simply nodded.

"Hello," answered Gabe, shyly.

Bill introduced himself to André and Edith. André took Gabe's suitcase from the trunk and followed Edith and Gabe to the house.

They walked through the back door, through a porch and directly into the kitchen. The adults had already removed their soiled footwear and Edith helped Gabe with his. She invited everyone to sit at the kitchen table but Gabe was already busy playing with the family dog, who had followed them from outside. Two cats jumped into the fray, to Gabe's great pleasure.

Bill produced some official papers that required André and Edith's signatures, concluding the temporary foster placement of Gabe in their care. He explained the conditions and the financial arrangements, and provided a number of instructions and guidelines.

"The phone numbers you'll need to reach the Manitoba School are listed here," he said, pointing to one of the pages in the thick bundle. "We expect you to register him in a school program as soon as possible to give him a chance to integrate within the class before summer."

André jumped in eagerly. "We've already been talking to the school in Notre-Dame-de-Lourdes. There is a special needs teacher who would be very happy to have Gabriel join her class."

André and Edith read the most important papers, glanced over others and provided the information required for the government to mail their monthly allowance cheque. Bill carefully reviewed the remuneration schedule, which provided for room and board, clothing, entertainment, and an annual allowance to send their foster child to camp.

As Edith offered the men coffee and biscuits she had baked, the little boy from Lilac Cottage had already made himself at home in the living room, facing the dark screen of the television, playing with the dog and cats. Edith watched him polish off his own plate of cookies and gulp the milk, barely taking the time to breathe.

"More?" she inquired.

"Yes please!" answered Gabe. He had learned manners at the Manitoba School. He would learn much more during his time on the Boissy farm, where he would live with Edith, her husband, and their three older children, Monique, Patrick, and Annie.

Bill stepped into the living room to say goodbye. Gabe ran to him. The nurse caught him in mid-stride and lifted him to the ceiling, as high as his strong arms could reach. "I'm going to miss you little guy. You have been a great source of joy and pride for me and for everyone else who looked after you," he told Gabe. "I know you'll be happy here." As he lowered Gabe, he gave him a hug.

"Goodbye, Mr. Milburn," was all Gabe said.

Gabe waved from the kitchen window, watching Bill drive away. The smoke from the exhaust pipe hung in the air a little longer, and then dissipated in the shadows of the tall oak trees. With it, a page turned on a successful two and a half years in Portage la Prairie. Gabe had yet to discover what an important new chapter was beginning—still away from his little sister, Claudette, his brothers, his mom, and his dad, but closer to some surprising developments.

Surprise

The phone rang on Hull Avenue, in Winnipeg. Angélina picked it up.

"*Allô!*"

"Angélina, you'll never guess who is in my class." Angélina recognized the voice of her friend, Sister Georgette.

"Who?" she asked.

"Angélina, Gabriel is in my class!" announced Sister Georgette.

"*Pas possible!*" exclaimed Angélina. Could it be that her prayers had been answered? "But how can that be? Isn't he in Portage?" asked Angélina, grasping the significance of the news. This was a complete surprise.

It appears that arrangements for fostering Gabe were completed without an opportunity to discuss the matter with Angélina and Louis, contrary to the recommendation written in Gabe's final evaluation report. These things happened.

We had to go to Notre-Dame-de-Lourdes for registration in a special class. To my big happy surprise, the teacher was Sister Georgette Pantel. She was my Mom's best friend! So as soon as we were gone, she phoned my Mom to tell her that she would be teaching me all the basics like speaking, reading, math, and spelling.

She said to my Mom: "What surprised me so much is that when she showed me the classroom and the library, I looked at a few books, I chose one, sat on the floor, and started looking at the pages... I think he really was reading it. There was not lots of pictures in it but was a funny story and I could see him smile away. You know, I don't think it's going to be that hard to get him to speak, just with a lot of love and attention."

—Gabe's scribbler

"Don't you worry," Sister Georgette said. "I will work very hard with him. I will keep in touch and tell you of the progress we are making."

Sister Georgette explained that Gabe had been sent to live with a foster family, in Treherne, and would be attending school in Notre-Dame-de-Lourdes. She assured Angélina that the Boissy family were very nice and they would surely take very good care of Gabe.

Georgette promised to get Angélina the Boissy's phone number, before saying goodbye. She hung up. Angélina kept the phone to her ear for what seemed like an eternity, listening to the continuous monotone signal, hypnotized. Eventually she replaced the phone in the cradle and sat down. Although surprised, a kind of serenity took hold of her—a renewed hope for Gabe, that one day he would return home.

Divine intervention?

Thus it was that Gabe, a resident of the Manitoba School for Retardates, was placed under the supervision of the Boissy family, in Treherne, and attended a special needs class in Notre-Dame-de-Lourdes, taught by Sister Georgette Pantel, a close friend of Gabe's mother. But how does Gabe end up in Treherne, and not in Dauphin, Beausejour, Brandon, or Morden? Was Gabe's move to Treherne a coincidence? Happenstance? Divine intervention? Or does a simple and rational explanation exist?

Everyone loves a good mystery. Nothing in Gabe's file, or the multitude of conversations, provides any evidence that this was a planned, arranged and coordinated outcome.

Angélina leans toward a divine intervention. "Somebody up there was looking out for Gabe and his family." She smiles.

Dr. Lowther remembers that "any official administrative measure initiated by the Manitoba School should have been recorded in Gabe's personal file." Yet, no record concerning the move to the Boissy family exists in the file.

Edith Boissy is unequivocal; she did not request specifically to have Gabe as a foster child in her home. Angélina is just as insistent: "I did

Sister Georgette Pantel

not make a special request for Gabe to attend Sister Georgette's class, let alone have him fostered in the Notre-Dame-de-Lourdes area." This leaves us wondering if Sister Georgette might have had something to do with it. Unfortunately, since Sister Georgette passed away in 2003, she cannot help us shed light on the mystery today. But her relatives give a few hints.

Sister Georgette's nephew, Roger Pantel, was the principal at Notre-Dame-de-Lourdes Elementary School that spring when Gabe enrolled. Today he is a jovial older gentleman with piercing blue-grey eyes—the kind that once could see right through his students and his teachers, when he was the principal.

Asked about the seemingly impossible concert of circumstances that brought Gabe to his school, including the long friendship between Sister Georgette and Angélina, Roger smiled at the question. He felt like a character in a detective story.

"My aunt could be very persuasive. I wouldn't be surprised one bit if she would have had conversations with the right people in Portage la Prairie to make this happen. But I have no knowledge of this."

Denise Bélisle, one of Georgette's nieces and a former teacher herself, revealed that her aunt was very competitive. This applied to how Georgette played cards. But everyone who knew her agrees that this also applied to how she did her work and how she lived her life. Could it have also applied to the efforts she might have deployed to bring Gabe to her class and see him succeed?

Neither Roger nor Denise could say for sure what motivated their aunt to devote much of her life to teaching children with special needs. But Denise offered a small detail that provides a possible clue.

"I remember that Georgette's parents and my parents participated in Faith and Light Communities, in Winnipeg, in Somerset and in Lourdes."

Denise explains that these were groups concerned with helping those less fortunate individuals in the community, primarily people with mental disabilities.

"Faith and Light was born of a desire to help people with an intellectual disability and their families find their place within the Church and society." She refers to a 1971 pilgrimage to Lourdes, France, which, at the urging of Jean Vanier, stimulated the formation of Faith and Light.

The clues from Sister Georgette herself might come from a self-evaluation questionnaire she filled out in 1983, part of the regular performance evaluation process the Chanoinesses followed. Her answers reveal Georgette's feelings concerning her work with special needs students during her teaching career.

"It gives me real joy to realize that I am important in the eyes of these children," she said. "I learn a great deal by working with them: their wonderful simplicity, humility, spontaneity and respect."

Asked to provide reasons for wanting to continue this vocation, Sister Georgette wrote, "The work is extremely worthwhile and provides many opportunities to deal with parents, teachers and other adults. My influence with other children in the school can have many other positive consequences. To forget myself, to give of myself, help me grow."

Finally it is back to Dr. Lowther for a final word on the matter. The question is asked point blank: "How likely is it that Sister Georgette would have talked with someone on your staff—Gabe's social worker for example—and arranged to have him fostered with the Boissy family, to allow her to teach him?"

"I would say it is more than likely. These conversations happened often. Otherwise it just makes too many things happen simply by coincidence, which would have required all the planets to line up."

It seems that every good story needs a hero. In the case of Gabe's placement at Treherne, Sister Georgette earns the title.

DANCING GABE
91

CHAPTER 11

Life on the Farm

> We all have possibilities we don't know about. We can do things we don't even dream we can do.
>
> —*Dale Carnegie*

Meanwhile, once Angélina learned that Gabe had been taken in by André and Edith Boissy, and had obtained their phone number, she eagerly contacted Edith to introduce herself and ask about her son. The first call surprised Edith. However, being a mother herself, she appreciated and understood Angélina's plight. Gabe remained under the charge of the department of Social Services, the responsibility of the Manitoba School, and yet a mother had a right to know what was going on.

Soon, Angélina would call regularly to inquire about Gabe and talk with him briefly. She was glad to know that Gabe was happy, cared for, and treated as a genuine member of the Boissy family.

How she longed to have him home, beside her, back where he belonged!

Living on the farm had its advantages, Gabe learned. Wide open spaces to play and run. Nature to explore and learn. Animals to discover, observe, care for, and even play with. Great food: fresh eggs, milk, cream, butter, vegetables, fresh fruits in season, meat at every meal, fresh bread, and baking. Very little noise, traffic, and people. Forest and fields as far as the eye could see for a playground. Freedom.

Life on the farm came with its hardships as well. There was always lots of work to be done, every day, for everyone. Groceries and errands required long drives, sometimes in difficult conditions. The usual comforts or convenience of city life shined by their absence, like having to go to the pump for drinking water, or using the outhouse, the honey-bucket in the basement, or at night, the chamber pot because the house was not equipped with indoor plumbing in Gabe's first year there.

"We used the phone book for toilet paper at the time Gabe moved here. Eventually we bought real toilet paper, a treat!" Edith Boissy explains that the phone book was quite an improvement over the Sears catalogue she had used in her grandmother's outhouse.

For refrigeration, Edith says, the family used an "ice hut." "The men would go and cut slabs of ice on nearby lakes—Pinkerton Lakes were only about a mile away—and haul them back in the truck." The ice slabs were stored beneath the wood floor of the ice hut, covered in saw dust. "That's where we would keep the meat, milk and cream, things that I prepared, and all other perishables."

Morning routine in the Boissy household included a breakfast consisting mostly of his favourite cereal—Gabe recalls he really liked Sugar Crisp, "the bear on the bicycle cereal"—then, quickly brushing teeth, washing face, and getting dressed. Routine has always been important for Gabe.

Milking cows, cooking meals, chores, the garden, laundry, dishes —Gabe did his part around the house. In the kitchen, he liked to dry the dishes as Annie washed them. Gabe also made it his job to walk the pail of kitchen scraps out and spill its contents about the pigpen.

Edith would always take the kids along when she did chores. With too many things around the house tempting kids to get in trouble, taking no chances was the prudent way.

"Sometimes they stayed [and played] in the manger," she explains. "I had to milk the cows by hand."

"I tried to milk the cows but it was very hard. Mrs. Boissy was an expert at it," Gabe says with a respectful tone. "We always had fresh milk. It was so good."

> *We were up early in the morning. There was lots of pretty hard work to do. They had cows and chickens, cats, and two dogs. They had a big field and Mrs. Boissy had a nice big garden...*
>
> —Gabe's scribbler

The Boissys had a big garden with lots of potatoes to satisfy the family's "meat and potatoes" diet. Gabe would fill pails of water at the well and carry them to the garden, where his foster mother waited, always thankful for the extra help. He also enjoyed picking apples. Annie, Patrick and Gabe also enjoyed stopping by the hen house to collect fresh eggs. They loved to spend time in the chicken brooder to watch and play with the little chicks.

André Boissy drove the school bus that brought country students to Notre-Dame-de-Lourdes and back. On school days, his yellow school bus left the yard at the same time every day, immediately after breakfast, and Gabe knew to be on it, sitting in the same seat every day.

Annie remembers Gabe's large appetite. "He loved his food, wasn't fussy. He always asked for seconds."

"The kid was like a bottomless pit," Edith adds, laughing.

The Boissy family farm in Treherne (circa 1972). Courtesy of the Boissy family.

The Boissy house would be filled with the wonderful aroma of bread baking in the oven every Saturday morning. Gabe enjoyed the routine of filling in as Edith's baking assistant on Saturday mornings.

"I would give the kids their own ball of dough to knead," explains Edith with a smile. "Gabe just loved it! He would roll his ball, and roll it some more, until it was perfect. And he would give it to me to put with the rest of the loaves as they sat, waiting for the yeast to do its job."

Edith would put all of the kids' creations into the oven. Gabe would sit by the oven, waiting for his round loaf to be ready, taking in the warmth of the oven and the smell of homemade bread. Everyone would wait expectantly, listening to Edith's timer tick away the seconds, watching the pointer inch its way closer to the top of the clock, and finally jump at the sound of the bell.

"Oh, it was so funny," Edith recalls. "Once baked, Gabe's ball was hard as a rock. He always rolled it so tight."

Edith would tell them all to sit at the table, concerned that they might get burned by the hot stove door. She would take every golden loaf out of its pan and use her brush to apply a liberal coat of farm-fresh butter. Everyone sat, wide-eyed, mouths watering.

Eventually, when the first batch of loaves had cooled sufficiently, Edith would place a loaf on the cutting board and look at her husband.

It was the signal everyone waited for. Under Gabe's watchful eye, André would take the serrated bread knife and apply it gently to the golden crust. He would tap the blade to the crust like a maestro taps his baton to get the orchestra's attention, music to Gabe's ears. Then he would work the blade back and forth, slowly, until the blade split the crust and steam rose from the loaf. This magical moment captivated the kids. Soon the first slice would be lying on the cutting board. Edith would butter it and hand it to Gabe. What a treat!

Gabe particularly enjoyed riding on the combine and the farm tractor with André, who farmed oats, wheat and barley. He would also ride in the truck, hauling grain with André. Gabe joined the family on car rides to Morden, Carman, and Winkler to 4-H Club meetings. Patrick would take him to the pasture, on the back of the Kawasaki 90 motorcycle, to herd the cows back to the barn. Plenty of action to keep a teenager busy.

One day I saw a ladder near the rack of hay. Stacks of hay indeed. I climbed it and once I was on top, jumping off was a lot of fun, but I slipped and fell off. Boom! I broke my arm. They took me to Notre-Dame Hospital. The doctor put my arm in a cast and I went back to the house. I had to sit on the sofa and watch TV. It was painful for a long time.

—Gabe's scribbler

Watching TV was not allowed at meal times in the Boissy household. But Edith remembers vividly how André would get up after dinner to watch TV—never sports. "Gabi would be right beside him. They were inseparable, those two."

To keep Gabe occupied, Edith had purchased the World Book Encyclopaedia. "I'm sure that Gabe read through every page, more than once," Edith recalls with a mother's pride. Daughter Annie remembers Gabe's amazing knowledge of geography, especially Manitoba's.

Tiny, the Chihuahua

The Boissy family dog, a Chihuahua named Tiny, loved to play with Gabe. He was a patient pet that would never get mad, growl or bark. Except once, recalls Annie.

The entire family sat in the living room, watching TV. Tiny lay on the rug, beside Gabe. That's when Gabe decided to challenge the little dog.

"Bite me, Tiny! Bite me!" Gabe would say. But, try as he may, Tiny would not move, his small pointy nose aimed directly at the TV, mesmerized.

"Bite me, Tiny! Bite me!" Gabe insisted. Again, Tiny would not bite.

Gabe, at his wit's end, bent down on all fours beside the Chihuahua, the dog paying little attention to him. That soon changed when, getting closer yet, with his best dog imitation, Gabe moved his head closer to Tiny's tail and bit it gently. Gabe had finally succeeded in drawing the dog into his game.

Tiny barked and jumped. Gabe was already on the move.

"I've never seen a kid run so fast," recalls Annie.

Gabe raced up the stairs to his bedroom, Tiny on his heels, barking, and snapping. As the dog caught up to his young assailant, all the Boissys could hear was a mix of childish laughter and happy canine yipping and yapping. Fortunately for Gabe, he never tried this with the family's two pet racoons.

Gabe felt at home with his new family and got used to his new routine. The Manitoba School for Retardates soon became a distant memory. He had a new family, his second family.

At the end of the initial probation period, Gabe's stay with the Boissy family was extended. It would be extended four more times over the next two years.

The Boissy family received a total of $74.00 per month from the Manitoba government for looking after Gabe.

"I had to give him seven dollars as an allowance for treats," Edith explains, with emphasis, "to be spent foolishly." One Sunday, he didn't get his treat, an ice cream cone, because he was chuckling in church and being disruptive." Apparently, Gabe was quite fond of treats and ice cream back then, and the light punishment proved effective.

During his two and a half years with the Boissy family, Gabe was the subject of a number of letters and varying orders governed by the province's Mental Health Act. The administrative processes of the provincial department of health and social services, and of the Director of Child Welfare, ensured that the responsibility for Gabe was always well documented and up to date. The net result was that Gabe lived with the Boissy family, was well cared for, and attended school in Notre-Dame-de-Lourdes.

Visitors for Gabe

When Gabe's siblings found out that he had been sent to live with another family, in Treherne, they were confused and angry. Who could blame them? After all, when you are six, seven, eight, eleven or twelve—age is pretty much irrelevant in this situation—how are you supposed to understand?

"Why is he there?" the kids would continually ask Angélina, when the subject of their brother Gabe come up in the conversation. "Why can't he come home?"

Angélina would usually avoid answering this question, afraid her kids would realize the pain she felt inside. She missed Gabriel immensely—he had been away for almost three years—and wanted him by her side. However, she was most pleased with the progress Gabe made in Portage. She knew that Sister Georgette's teaching would benefit Gabe and maybe even allow him to come home, for good. Thankfully, until that time came, the Langlois were allowed to visit Gabe at the farm on a few occasions, often chauffeured by Angélina's brothers or nephews.

"I liked the animals," Claudette remembers, "but I didn't really understand what was 'wrong' with Gabe, and why he couldn't live with us. I was only seven at the time."

Angélina remembers of one particular visit in late summer, along with Mike and Claudette.

The kids were soon invited to set out and sail on the small pond, on a raft that André had made for them, mainly of foam and wood. The embarkation had kept two or three kids afloat before, but with the new sailors on board, it soon began to list and take on water. With much screaming and splashing, the little raft rocked back and forth, adapting to the motion of each one of its passengers. Mike, looking to break rafting speed records, stood at the stern of the raft, planted a long pole on the bottom of the slough and pushed with all his might, to every passenger's delight. The others, seated helter-skelter on the raft's deck, used their hands to row and propel their craft even faster. Concerned only with going faster, everyone had forgotten about navigating the ship.

Mike gave one last push. A second later, the raft came to an abrupt stop, running aground on the far side of the pond. The sudden impact surprised every little passenger, who screamed even louder. The rebound rocked the raft one more time. Mike lost his balance but tried to steady himself using the pole he was still holding.

"Oh, oh," he said. The other little crewmates turned just in time to see Mike fall overboard with a splash. A loud cheer echoed across the little pond, much to the amusement of André, who was keeping an eye on the children, from the shore.

A bunch of tired and soaked kids made their way off the raft and onto dry land. Edith and Angélina were waiting for them with towels, a pitcher of Kool-Aid, and a plate of homemade cookies.

"Mom, can I stay here for a day or two?" Mike asked. "Annie and Patrick said I could. I would look after Gabe too."

Angélina turned to Edith. "That would be fine with us. I can bring him to Winnipeg on Monday when I bring grain to town," she told Angélina, raising a cheer from the kids.

Sister Georgette's class

Gabe calls his encounter with Sister Georgette the "turning point of his life," and his mother agrees wholeheartedly. As an educator, Sister Georgette provided Gabe with the skills, the confidence, and the self-esteem he needed to succeed in life. She allowed him to develop to a point where he could rejoin his family, reintegrate with his community of St. Vital, and grow up to live a fulfilling life. Sister Georgette, and the

I really liked school every day; I learned something new and my teacher was very good. I live on a farm so every morning I had to take a bus to school and at 3:30 pm, in the bus, back to the house [farm]. Yes! There was Notre-Dame Elementary School, and across the street, Notre-Dame High School. I remember watching the kids programs such as Chez Helene, Mister Dress-Up with Casey and Finnegan, Ernie Coombs. The Friendly Giant (Look way up! Rusty and Jerome the Giraffe). Sesame Street (Oscar the Grouch, Big Bird, Kermit the Frog, Grover, Ernie and Bert). Mr. Hooper running the General Store. Bob McGrath singing. Numbers 1 through 10 or 1 through 20, it doesn't really matter. Letters A to Z; who really knows the alphabet? It was great!

We followed exercise programs on TV, such as yoga, Jack LaLane (the man who says breathe in and breathe out). He is still alive today. He does the juicer infomercials. And there's Ed Allen. He used to exercise outside in Jamaica, live. At the end of the show, quote/unquote: "Don't forget to do your homework!" We did all that at school, in the morning, to keep fit.

Sister Georgette taught me how to read (Read the directions). Writing; the Write Stuff and it's excellent. Arithmetic, as in Mathematics—"Math" for short. Times tables was such an easy thing to do: ten in a row. Addition, you can add it up with pluses; subtraction can take it away with the minuses; multiplication, you multiply by the times and carry the numbers you want; division, who divides by numbers. She taught me to read little books and big books. I learned the continents such as North America, South America, Europe, Asia, and Australia. I've done the rest of the world—I meant the maps of the world. I've listened and I'm pretty good at knowing it all...

—Gabe's scribbler

others who taught Gabe, ensured he developed a solid set of social skills that would serve him well for the rest of his life.[17]

Principal Roger Pantel, Georgette's nephew, left his position as principal at the end of the 1972 school year and returned to Winnipeg, where he took a teaching position in St. Vital (he would eventually teach Mike and Rick a few years later). At his leaving, teachers and students at Notre-Dame organized a farewell celebration.

Now, in 2014, Roger shows off a scrapbook prepared by the students under the guidance of Sister Georgette and the other teachers. "Farewell, Mr. Principal" is written on the cover, a yellowed page with darkened and frayed edges, adorned by the picture of a bouquet of roses; a fine tribute and souvenir of his tenure in Notre-Dame.

Roger shows the message on the front, his blue eyes glistening. The hand-written message in French is by Georgette. Her tone and eloquence are unmistakable, as is her handwriting:

"So long, good luck! This missive to our dear principal contains our tribute of tenderness and gratitude. On this serene day, be one hundred times happy—you so deserve it. Accept our present, which cannot express all that our hearts would like to say, but our wishes for happiness and future successes."

Roger saved a surprise, the real reason for showing the scrapbook, a treasure he has safeguarded. He flips through the yellowed pages, careful not to tear their weathered and brittle paper until he stops at a lined page with signatures and discoloured pieces of brittle Scotch tape. "That's Gabe's class," he says.

All the names on the page, save one, are written in elegant cursive letters. The teachers' names—Sister Georgette Pantel and Bernard Balcaen—in red ink; the students' names signed in blue or black ink. The script signature beside Roger's index finger: Gabriel Langlois.

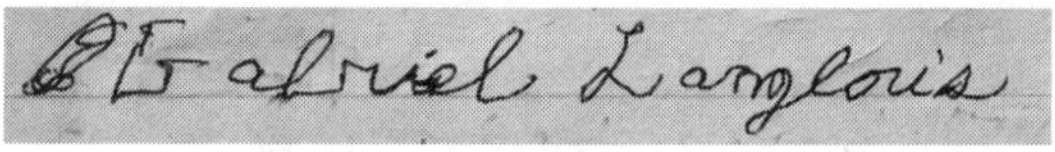

"You know," he recalls, "one day at École Lavallée, [several years later in Winnipeg], I was outside at recess and this strapping young man walks directly toward me. He stops a few feet away, towering over me and extends his hand. As I shake his hand, I recognize him. He says with a smile and an uncommon assurance: 'You are Roger Pantel. You left Notre-Dame in 1972.' It was Gabe. He had changed; this was a man standing in front of me. I've never forgotten that time."

Roger knows the Langlois family well, having taught brothers Mike and Rick, having socialized with Louis, and having met Angélina on several occasions.

"I think for Angélina, her family has always been her reason for living, for fighting, and for surviving."

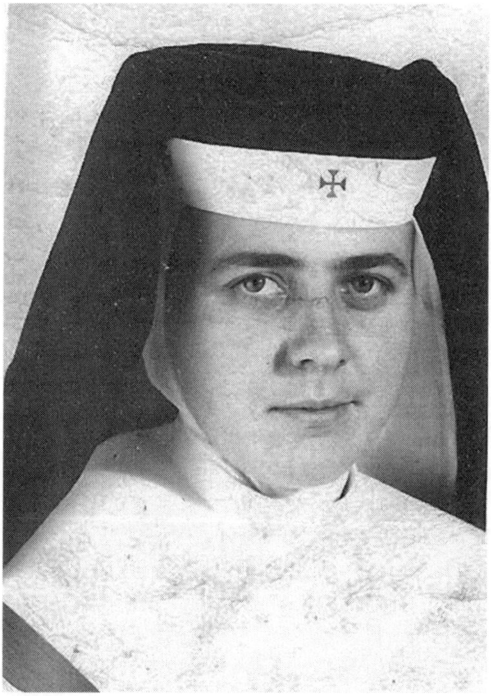

Sister Marie-Augustine (Georgette Pantel), 1953.
Courtesy of Denise Bélisle.

HALF-TIME

Sister Georgette Pantel

Sister Georgette was sharp like a bell!
—*Edith Boissy*

"She was a second mother for those kids," says Roger Pantel, Sister Georgette's nephew. "If kids were hungry, she wouldn't hesitate to take them to the convent across the street to get them something to eat. If kids came to school dirty, or had soiled themselves during the day, she wouldn't hesitate to take them to the convent and give them a bath."

Angélina Langlois recalls Georgette telling her specifically about how she cared for Gabe. "She noticed Gabe eating chalk in class one day, and concluded that he was hungry. She assumed that he was not eating sufficiently at home, and shared her concerns with me and asked permission to feed Gabe at the convent. But only after she had received Mother Superior's permission to do so."

At the time, Edith Boissy had been concerned about Gabe's weight. According to her daughter Annie, Edith would give Gabe a smaller plate, which was always full but with reduced portions. While he always asked for seconds, that never seemed to be enough food for Gabe. Sister Georgette's attentions kept him satiated, but probably did not help control his weight.

Like Angélina, Georgette Pantel's compassion was well rooted in her upbringing. She was born in Notre-Dame-de-Lourdes on September 27,

1927, daughter of Jean-Baptiste and Berthe (nee Deletrez). She grew up on the family farm until the age of twelve, when her parents decided to move to town.

Pursuing her interest in education and teaching, Georgette Pantel joined the Chanoinesses Régulières des Cinq Plaies in 1944—the same order Angélina would join two years later. Three years later she began her long and productive teaching career in Winnipeg. Later she would teach in St. Lupicin, St. Leon, Haywood, Winnipeg, and again in Notre-Dame-de-Lourdes on a number of occasions. Gabe was enrolled in her class during her five-year stint teaching mentally and physically handicapped children from 1970 to 1975. She concluded her teaching career in Lourdes, teaching religion to high school students.

Sister Georgette's Teacher Evaluation Form of February 21, 1973, provides insights into her work with special needs students.

> Sister Georgette is able to create a healthy learning environment. Her students are comfortable and feel accepted as they are; Sister Georgette demonstrates the utmost respect toward each of them.
>
> Her control of the class is "magnifique" considering the students with whom she works. Sister Georgette follows her students closely, each of them being an individual with a particular problem... She does not hesitate to try new methods to help her students.

Sister Blandine Chaput, the Chanoinesses' Mother Superior General, similarly summed up Sister Georgette's career, in her "obedience letter":

> You demonstrate toward them the tenderness of Jesus Christ, whom you help them to discover, day after day, by who you are and what you do. Your influence also reaches the parents and other teachers, to whom you bring hope, light and courage. As such, you continue a work of teaching faith, a tangible work anchored in your everyday actions."

Annette Bosc, the mother of one of Sister Georgette's students, remembers her as strict and tenacious, while also patient and understanding toward her students. Annette greatly appreciated Sister Georgette's sense of humour during Gilbert's four years at the school in Somerset. She recalls an amusing anecdote to exemplify Georgette's cheerful nature.

"On his First Communion, Gilbert noticed Sister Georgette in one of the pews, just as he received the host [communion wafer]. Much to my horror, with the host in his hand and a broad smile on his face, Gilbert waved ("with the host!" Mrs. Bosc emphasizes) at Sister Georgette, who waved back affectionately."

The children returned to their pews. Gilbert took his place beside his mom, obviously displeased with her son's behaviour. But Gilbert spoke first, before Annette could think of something to say.

"Mom, I have Jesus in my heart!"

Gilbert left his mother speechless.

When she shared her horror with Sister Georgette on her way out of the church, she reassured Annette.

"Mais c'est correct! But it's alright!" she explained with her broad smile. "It would have been rude not to say hi to his favourite teacher."

Annette remembers Sister Georgette regularly inquiring about Gilbert after he had moved on. "You know, Sister Georgette always maintained an interest in her students' progress and success."

Bernard Balcaen taught the other special needs class at Notre-Dame-de-Lourdes Elementary School, at the same time as Sister Georgette. He echoes everyone's sentiments.

"She was so good, gentle, kind, humble," he says. "She had such a maternal instinct. She saw her role as much more than a teacher. She was everyone's favourite."

Bernard helps us understand the experience of teaching children with special needs in a small rural setting, more than forty years ago.

"It was not easy. With seven or eight students to a class, each with his or her own needs. We taught mathematics, reading, spelling and

Sr. Georgette, November 1989. Courtesy of Denise Bélisle.

geography. It was important for us to teach them life skills as well. We also involved them in physical education to the limit of their abilities. We did not give homework to the kids; we knew that parents already had plenty to do when the kids got home."

Bernard's parting words emphasize Sister Georgette's devotion.

"She was always ready and eager to lend a hand, to anyone. She was strict, her students knew it, but she was fair. I think for Sister Georgette, it was a personal mission: she was always there for her students."

Bernard shares one last thought, with a smile: "Sister Georgette loved to laugh. I think everyone would agree that she was *'à la mode'* (she was 'with it'), for a nun, she even drove her own car."

Sister Georgette must have made quite an impression behind the wheel of her car because Roger mentioned it as well, in somewhat more precise terms. "Yes, I remember she drove. She booted it, a bit of a lead foot," he says with a hearty laugh—just one of the many changes brought about by Vatican Council II.

After her retirement in 1992 Sister Georgette served as pastoral care worker, visiting and distributing communion to the sick. As a result, she often led prayers at the funerals of the same persons she accompanied in their illness

After she fell ill to pancreatic cancer, those closest to her say, Georgette became quite sombre, even angry, and at times afraid, that her Lord had chosen to come and get her while she still had so much left to do. "Why me?" is a question she repeated many times, according to her niece, Denise.

"She was not ready to die," asserts a former colleague, Sister Florence Vuignier. "She felt that her mission was unfinished." But she had done so much, for others.

Sister Georgette died on October 10, 2003, at the Notre-Dame Hospital, at the age of 76. As an article in the community newspaper noted, "*Les actions de Soeur Georgette ont parlé fort.*" The actions of Sister Georgette spoke volumes.

Roger Pantel adds, "I don't think my aunt would have necessarily realized the magnitude of her contribution, the impact she had on the lives of her students. When I think of Gabe, I see Georgette's work and I imagine how proud she would be of him."

SECOND HALF THRIVING

THIRD QUARTER

NO PLACE LIKE HOME

CHAPTER 12

Going Back to Winnipeg

Family is not an important thing. It's everything.
—*Michael J. Fox*

At the end of the school year, early in the summer of 1974, Georgette told Angélina that she felt Gabe was ready to go home and attend regular school. Angélina and Louis discussed bringing Gabe home to stay.

"I told Louis that Georgette was sure that Gabe could live with us and go to school, just like his brothers and sister. He said 'Ok.' I don't think I gave him a choice," she adds with a laugh.

Angélina later raised the issue with Edith Boissy, who understood that Angélina wanted her son at home. Reluctantly, she brought the issue to the attention of staff at the Manitoba School. Much to Angelina's excitement, Gabe's caseworker met with her and Edith to discuss the possibility of having Gabe reintegrate with his family.

Understandably, Edith's reacted to the prospect with mixed emotions. Gabe had grown fond of her and André, and their three children. They considered him a genuine member of their family.

"He even called me Mom," Edith recalls, misty-eyed. "I really loved the little guy like my own. He was a wonderful kid. It ripped me apart to see him leave." She pauses as she collects herself. "But I understood he had to get back to his family."

Edith had to face the reality that two of her children would leave the house at the end of that summer. Her oldest, Monique, was marrying in July, and Gabe would return to Winnipeg. The joy of seeing her oldest start a new life of her own would be dampened by the sorrow of losing Gabe, not yet a teenager, who would also begin anew.

Angélina and Edith arranged to bring Gabe home at the end of the school year. However, when Gabe was told of this, he became quite upset. He had not been trained to deal with such a sudden rush of emotions. The routine he had developed over the past two years was being disrupted, dramatically.

Gabe wanted to go home, but he was most disturbed at the possibility of missing Monique's wedding, to which he had been invited—a most distinguished guest. He made such a fuss that Angélina had to reassure and console him. Everyone soon agreed that Gabe would stay in Treherne until after the wedding. Angélina even sent him some money to buy a present for Monique—a pretty set of dishes."

Monday, July 8, 1074

Accompanied by her nephew, Angélina drove to Treherne, on July 8, 1974, and brought Gabe home, without making much of a fuss, for fear of upsetting Gabe. "I only brought him home with the clothes on his back. I didn't want him to be frightened. But I was ready to have him at home with me. It was time," said Angélina.

Gabe had visited his family previously, on weekends or for holidays, and therefore his return to Winnipeg did not raise suspicions at home—at least for a little while—that another important change was taking place. However, as days passed and Gabe enjoyed the rest of the summer with his family, his siblings could sense a difference. The Langlois family was whole, again. Angélina's prayers had been answered.

"Getting him back home was the best thing we could do," says Gerry.

On October 3rd, 1974, the final Varying Order was signed, officially returning Gabe to his parents' care, even though Gabe actually returned to his family on July 8, in time to enjoy the summer holidays with his siblings, and get ready for school. It seems Gabe couldn't wait for the bureaucracy. The order read:

> "[...] I hereby order that Gabriel Langlois be discharged from the supervision of Mrs. Boissy and be placed under the care and supervision of his parent, Mrs. Angélina Langlois... St. Vital, Winnipeg, Manitoba, effective September 16, 1974."

My Dad bought our house in St. Vital, on Hull Avenue, in 1969, where we've lived ever since. I love my house; it was the best place ever. My Mom work very hard with all the cleaning, working, ironing, the cooking, oh she made her own bread, buns, and cookies. Oh! That was so good.

—Gabe's scribbler

CHAPTER 13

Gabe's Years in the Public School System

To be yourself in a world that is constantly trying to make you something else is the greatest accomplishment.

—*Ralph Waldo Emerson*

"I rejoined the family; I was absolutely ecstatic!" Gabe bellows in an interview. "It's a little bit emotional for me to talk about this."

Then he becomes matter-of-fact. "That year [1974] was Winnipeg's centennial, you know. It was great to have a room, even if I shared it with Rob. We had bunk beds."

In August, Gabe attended a day camp at St. George School, where he participated in plays and played tag and baseball." Meanwhile, as September approached, Gabe's parents enrolled him at Softley School for children with special needs. This was to be a very short stay, however. Gabe found it frustrating trying to adapt to this new program.

Angélina then decided to contact the principal at Christ the King, a parochial school one block from the Langlois home. Sister Marcia Stanley, the principal at the time, told Angélina that she would need to consult with her staff.

Margaret Kingdon, Gabe's Grade 6 teacher, remembers the discussion between the principal and a few teachers who would be responsible for Gabe. They reached a unanimous agreement in very little time—another key decision in Gabe's journey to success.

It was with a broad smile and overwhelming joy that Angélina exclaimed to the family at the dinner table: "They said yes! Gabe can be in the normal school system. He will be going to Christ the King!"

Gabe would attend three schools during the next eight years, eventually earning his high school diploma.

Christ the King School years

Gabe recounts fond memories of his grade five and six years at Christ the King. In doing so, he starts with food, which often seems to be a priority for him. "Mom made my lunch: sandwiches and cookies. Sometimes I would get money to buy hot dogs." But sometimes Gabe would go home for lunch and watch television.

He remembers the name of many classmates and friends with whom he played football, spent time at recess, or did homework. Of course, Gabe also remembers the name of every teacher.

"The teacher introduced me as Gabriel but the kids all called me Gabe. I had good friends at Christ the King; I didn't hang out with bad kids. I always felt part of the gang."

"I remember Caroline Newenberg. She helped me with the metric system—that was difficult. I also remember Laurie Salo, who taught music. I played Mary Had a Little Lamb on the recorder."

Gabe also remembers the fire drills. He was always prepared and he knew what to do when that bell rang. It is with a proud look that Gabe tells of his class winning a trophy in a fire drill competition in 1975.

According to his younger brother Rob, Gabe was a lot more "quirky" then, with his incessant hand gestures and talking to himself. "He had no attention span, but he didn't harm anyone."

Field trips were some of Gabe's favourite activities. He tells of a time in 1975 when they went to a choir event at Dakota Collegiate. Christ the King's group sang "Sing", a song kids would have heard at the time on Sesame Street, but popularized by The Carpenters.

"School was so easy," says Gabe. "Math, science, spelling, French, the Elevens table." Then he switches to a totally different topic without missing a beat.

"My favourite TV show back then was Archie and his Friends, with Marvin Mouse, Uncle Bob Swartz. It was great! We would run home for lunch, eat our lunch, and race to the TV to watch the show. Uncle Bob had a puppet named Archie, another named Marvin Mouse, and they would talk and entertain."[18]

Gabe explains that Uncle Bob became the mayor of Funtown, an eventual Archie and Friends spinoff.

A teacher remembers

Margaret Kingdon, Gabe's grade six teacher (she became Christ the King's principal the following year, a position she would occupy for the next eighteen years) remembers Gabe as "the most amazing student I have had the pleasure to teach. Today, I see him at hockey games and football games and I tell people, proudly, that I taught that kid!"

As one of a number of kids with intellectual disabilities at the school, Margaret remembered that Gabe's handicap was not a social barrier. "Of all the kids who were challenged, Gabe was really happy—always—and the kids really liked him... Baseball was the big thing at recess. He was on the team and they would give him as many pitches as he needed to hit the ball. Then they would say, 'Run Gabe! Run!... He had self-esteem, I could tell just from watching him during some events."

As for academics, Margaret recalls an official Ministry of Education IQ test conducted at various grade levels. From a first glance at Gabe's answer sheet, he appeared to have scored a perfect one hundred percent. But it turned out that Gabe had coloured all the circles on the multiple-choice questionnaire's answer sheet, so that when the marking mask was laid over the page, all the right answers showed through the perforations.

Gabe, nevertheless, was sharp. "In Grade 6," Margaret recalls, "he could read off the scale for Grade 12 students. He could read the words, but sometimes the comprehension may not have been there."

"He read a lot," brother Rick agrees. "Him and books. That's my most vivid memory of Gabe, with his nose either in a book or a magazine, always reading." Today, Gabe continues to spend hours reading books, magazines, the *Winnipeg Free Press* and the *Winnipeg Sun*.

"He never made a spelling mistake!" Margaret Kingdon continues. "And his handwriting, all cursives, was simply beautiful."

Margaret's memory of one particular Geography class discussion highlights the way some autistic minds work. "I explained that the head of The World Council of Churches was located in Geneva. I had barely mentioned the Swiss city when Gabe's hand shot up."

"Yes Gabriel," said Margaret, "you would like to share something with the rest of the class?"

"Red Cross Headquarters," Gabe told his classmates. He then provided details concerning the main diseases currently on the Red Cross list.

"He explained measles and the magnitude of the disease, then he went on to mumps and whooping cough. I was stunned and so proud of him. He had a photographic mind. He recited these facts verbatim, as if he was reading them directly from an encyclopaedia." That perception was likely accurate; on the farm in Treherne, he would have read the encyclopaedia several times over.

Another insight into Gabe's mind came when a student teacher read a picture book to the class. Wanting to confirm their understanding, she asked: "Tell me about the boy [in the story]," to which Gabe answered, "Red hair." This was followed by laughter from his classmates.

"The young intern was somewhat taken aback," Margaret said. "This was not one of the answers she was seeking, but it was a valid answer, nonetheless, and one that demonstrated Gabriel's attention to detail. Gabriel had taught me, and that young student teacher, an important lesson that I've carried with me to this day: Being clear and specific is most important when giving instructions, if you want to get the right result."

Holy Cross School years

According to Gabe's brothers and Angélina, Gabe developed his personality and began interacting more with the other students at Holy Cross, his junior high school. He had special friends of his own who would support him and cheer him on in the challenges he faced.

Gabe still remembers many of their names: Mark Hauser, Collette Mackenzie, Suzette McGibbon, Mark Carpenter with the British accent, and Anne Blonski. But his mood turns sombre as he remembers a tragedy. "One of the lowest moments of our lives was when Monique Brisebois, a classmate, was killed in a hit-and-run accident in the spring of 1977."

"The principal, Sister Alice, told everyone. It was quite sad," says Gabe.

School also provided many celebrative moments, and Gabe participated in those fully. He would never miss a school dance for example, and he would ask girls to dance with him.

Sister Alice Konefall, the principal at Holy Cross School at the time, recalls Gabe's years at the school vividly.

"Angélina came to me and asked if Gabriel could attend Holy Cross School. Holy Cross, at the time, was a private parochial school run mostly by sisters and financially supported by the parish. It had a good reputation for preparing kids well academically, socially and with faith-based values, motivating them to reach out and help others. Angélina explained that Gabriel had some learning disabilities and that he might require extra attention. I said 'Yes', but I wanted Gabriel to meet the teacher who might respond well to him, and meet the kids as well. Everyone would have to be part of the process to integrate Gabriel into the class."

Angélina was elated when permission was granted. As he did at Christ the King, Gabe flourished in the accepting atmosphere of the school.

"Gabe was very easygoing, friendly. He would pull out all of the sports statistics; his memory was stunning," Sister Alice recalls. One story is forever engraved in her memory.

"Gabe wanted to play basketball on the school team. He wasn't all that coordinated... but I felt he should have the chance, like any other kid. So I talked to Denis MacKenzie, the Phys. Ed. teacher. I don't know what he did, but one day I go to the gym [and saw that] Gabe was in the game, got a pass, took two or three dribbles, and shot... *nothing but net*!" Sister Alice is on the edge of her seat now, as everyone in the gymnasium was almost forty years ago, to describe the excitement as the ball swished through the basket without touching the rim.

"Everyone in the crowd—his classmates, his siblings, his relatives, and the players—gave him a standing ovation! He turned to the crowd and smiled with full teeth. You could see the joy!"

Sister Alice admits she learned from Gabe and from the other students. She learned to listen to them, recognize their gifts, and encourage them. "People with learning challenges usually have other gifts. Gabe's is to be a friend... I see fulfilment in him, a real sense of accomplishment. He knows the joy... of being who you are... and to heck with the rest of the world."

Glenlawn Collegiate years

In September 1978, after graduating from Holy Cross, Gabe moved to Glenlawn Collegiate. "I think that was the first time I started a school year by myself," Gabe says. He was quite nervous, especially because the first day of school was also Picture Day. However, his new classmates soon made him forget his nervousness.

He remembers making friends at Glenlawn; Gabe periodically interrupts himself to add more names to his list of friends, as he recalls events from his Glenlawn years. Asked about the low points of his time at Glenlawn, Gabe does not hesitate. "I stayed after school once or twice, I wasn't doing enough in Science. Then I had the measles during the winter of 1979 and I had to stay home for five or ten days. That was not a proud moment."

The high points, on the other hand, are many. The winter of 1979 saw Gabe get his first job, albeit unpaid, at 7-Eleven.

"I gained some useful work experience there," he states. "We did Junior Achievement. That was a highlight. Our project was about business and we researched products like nuts, fruits and all kinds of other stuff. I also participated in the entire Toastmasters program—about public speaking—when we prepared a speech about politics and sports. That was my first award." Gabe's yellowed Toastmasters International certificate is stored safely in his box of souvenirs. Quite an achievement for a kid who only started speaking at the age of ten.

The total solar eclipse on February 26, 1979, recorded in the school yearbook is also a highlight that Gabe will not forget. "We stayed in and watched TV, because the school staff didn't want people to get blinded by the light."

Early in June of 1979, Angélina received a letter signed by Brenda Yost, Deputy Assistant Superintendent of the School Division, informing her that next fall, Gabe would attend the Special Education program.

On his first day of Grade 11, therefore, he would meet a man who would devote much time and effort to Gabe over the next two years—Mr. Bob Sadler, Special Education teacher.

Gabe confides that "Special Ed. was a nice turnaround for me," but quickly moves to the topic of school dances and Freshie Day.

Someone who has known Gabe and his family since their move to Hull Avenue feels that the Glenlawn dances sparked Gabe's identity as Dancing Gabe.

> It was between '77 and '80 at a Glenlawn dance with a band, probably Harlequin. Gabe and another mentally challenged fellow were dancing in between sets and people started throwing money at them. At first I thought it was kind of sad but the family and Gabe were tickled pink as Gabe made off with quite the bounty that day. Thus Dancing Gabe was born and forever lives on in the hearts of sports fans of Winnipeg and Canada.[19]

Gabe received a total of seven awards during his grade eleven year, which ended in June 1980, including a special sports award he received at the Glenlawn annual sports banquet. The rest of the list included awards for Junior Achievement of Manitoba, Communication Skills, Home Economics, Shops Level 4, Typing, and Work Experience.

"I volunteered at Tache Nursing Home during the spring [of 1980]. I took the bus to get there. I organized the books in the nursing home's library, I sat and talked with the senior residents. I felt good because I was doing good."
—*Gabe*

Bob Sadler

Bob Sadler, now sixty-three, keeps fond memories of teaching Gabe in Glenlawn's special education class in grades eleven and twelve.

"There was no real curriculum to follow at that time," Bob says. "A committee developed the curriculum along with learning objectives and goals. I had eight or nine students in my class. Our initial assessment showed most kids could read and write at a grade three or grade four level. But every kid was different."

Bob taught every subject to his Grade 11 class, quite a mandate.

"Gabe's work was always perfect! He was obedient beyond belief. He was very quiet. I never had to worry about the work being done and handed in on time."

He explains that the education system for kids with special needs at high school assumed two categories of kids: educable mentally handicapped (EMH)—kids with an IQ between 55 and 70, and trainable mentally handicapped (TMH)–kids with an IQ below 55.[20] Gabe was in the first category.

Bob notes that the Langlois family was always interested and supportive, making Gabe feel good about himself. "The family didn't want Gabe singled out. They wanted to know that he was protected, but not treated differently. His mom was wonderful. They were the nicest family I've ever had to deal with."

Bob continues, "Gabe loved music. He also loved statistics," an interesting combination. "I would not hesitate to show him off to the other teachers," he adds.

Gabe's former teacher almost makes him sound too good to be true. Asked about some of Gabe's challenges, Bob gathers his thoughts for a second.

"Handling change wasn't easy for Gabe. Routine was very important for him," he admits, citing changes in schedule, changes in assignments, all kinds of changes. Gabe liked his routine. "The only time Gabe got upset was when you messed up his schedule."

But one memory seems particularly special to Bob.

"Gabe gave me a gift, a book for Christmas. I was so touched. I still have it."

> "I think everyone wanted him to succeed. Gabe's surroundings and the people around him made it possible for him to succeed.
> *—Jill Mathez, Gabe's high school classmate*

Gabe recalls Spirit Week, an annual school event where classes wear distinctive colours, participate in indoor and outdoor events including tug-of-war, bike races, and egg-dropping (in which contestants throw and catch raw eggs at increasing distances). Indoor games were also on the schedule.

Gabe remembers the Pep Rally with particular fondness.

"We won it in Grade 10, Grade 11 and Grade 12, with Joey, Scott and company," Gabe says proudly. "It was the highlight of our lives!"

Asked to list the highlights of his graduating year, he immediately remembers "December 9, 1980," but then pauses, searching for the event linked to that particular date. "That's the day John Lennon was assassinated by Robert D. Chapman. I liked Lennon and the Beatles. That was very sad."

But on a happier topic, he also recalls, "That was the year that the Blue Bombers celebrated 50 years."

Standing up for their brother

That fall was also when Gabe's brothers Mike and Rick got in trouble on Gabe's behalf. Protecting Gabe was always a primary concern for the siblings; they would not let people take advantage of him. So it was that Gabe's brothers noticed that Gabe would always come home famished. Mike's investigation revealed that a Glenlawn student was pilfering Gabe's lunch money. It took much coaxing and convincing for the brothers to get Gabe to admit to this, and when he did, he would not give the person's name. Even today, Gabe will not mention names, even though he remembers the story as if it was yesterday. "That doesn't help anything. Wouldn't be right," he says.

Finally, on a school day, brothers Mike and Rick took a stroll to Glenlawn Collegiate, just before the lunchtime bell. They positioned themselves in the hallway, around the corner, in full view of Gabe's locker. When the students filed out of class for their lunch break, the brothers saw Gabe saunter over to his locker, spin the dial on the lock and pull it open. A few seconds later, as he was reaching for things in his locker, another student happened by Gabe's locker and shoved him in there, demanding that he hand over his lunch money.

This was the only cue the brothers needed to jump into action. Mayhem ensued and the kid "got the beating he deserved," according to Mike. The melee was quickly dispersed, and the three Langlois brothers were called to the principal's office. The news of the incident quickly spread through the student body.

Principal Peter Derenchuk, and Vice Principal George Carsted called Bob Sadler in to inquire about his knowledge of the "beat-up," as it became known among students and staff. "I remember I was so pissed off!" Bob says. "More mad at myself for not knowing that this had been going on, that someone was bullying Gabe and stealing his lunch money. I told Peter I would take care of it."

"He was bullied in a few instances, and the school, and I, didn't take too kindly to it," recalls Bob, whose new role consists of coaching special needs students in the Louis Riel School Division and finding job placements for them. "But people didn't really understand. We've come a long way..."

That day, for their punishment, Mike and Rick were required to address a number of classes and explain that although Gabe is different, that is no reason to take advantage of him or to bully him.

But memories were short. A few months later, Gerry heard through the grapevine that kids had been stealing Gabe's lunch money at Junior's Restaurant, a favourite hangout for students just across the street from Glenlawn.

One Friday, at lunchtime, Gerry drove to Junior's in the St. Vital Sandblasting one-ton truck and gave the students until Monday to return the money. Enough said. The money was returned.

"Growing up was tough for Gabe," Gerry says. "Now, with people's increased awareness of mental disabilities, things have changed a lot. But still, some people treat them badly. They can be pretty inconsiderate."

Graduation

Gabe's Grade Twelve graduation took place at the beginning of summer, 1981. For the dinner and dance before the big day, he invited his brother Rick as his date. Gabe will never forget the evening at the Marlborough Hotel. "It was excellent, exciting! I danced all night long, until two in the morning. It was a blast!"

Then came the graduation ceremony. "I was so nervous about Grad," Gabe says. "I got so sick that I almost didn't make it. I guess I was just too nervous, but I survived."

Angélina recalls that Sister Georgette and Sister Marie-Lucille attended Gabe's graduation. They stopped by the house on Hull in the afternoon, prior to the ceremony. Seeing how Gabe was feeling sick to his stomach, Sister Marie-Lucille offered him some pills that would eventually settle his stomach and allow him to attend his graduation ceremony.

Several hours later, Gabriel J. Langlois received his High School Diploma and Department of Education Diploma. "It was the greatest day of my life," Gabe remembers. "Everyone was there: Mom, Dad, Claudette and my brothers."

Gabe tells of the pomp and circumstance, and the pride he felt as he received his certificate, dressed in cap and gown. He describes the handing out of plaques, awards, scholarships and bursaries, and certificates.

But soon, Gabe moves on to recalling other facts of that year. "That was the summer of the Royal Wedding, in July."

A proud Glenlawn alumnus

That summer, Gabe started working with his dad, performing a number of office duties and light shop assignments. He returned to Glenlawn in September for an extra year, to learn practical life skills and continue to develop his knowledge. Bob Sadler explains that Gabe, and every other special needs graduate, could have remained at Glenlawn until age twenty-one, "depending on the diagnosis, and if the family wanted."

But even after that year, Gabe wasn't finished with his alma mater. Since his graduation, he has kept up his perfect attendance at Glenlawn's Spirit Week. In 2007, Gabe, now known throughout Winnipeg as "Dancing Gabe" and clad in his very own Manitoba Moose jersey, jeans, and white runners, stepped out to the centre of the Glenlawn gymnasium in front of a screaming crowd of students, teachers, and parents.

To the beat of music blaring from the speakers, Gabe began kicking his feet, waving his arms, shuffling to the beat. After almost forty-five seconds, and with Gabe still going strong, one masked student joined Gabe, immediately followed by another student.

By the time Gabe had been out there for a minute, more students lined up behind him and increased the frenzy of the dance. One student even demonstrated his break dancing abilities, and a gymnast performed impressive tumbling routines.

"So we were all chillin' in the gym one fine Spirit Week day, then all of a sudden Soulja Boy came on and Dancin' Gabe starts doing his thang. Then everyone joined in :) We've got spirit, yes we do!"[21]

Tuesday, June 11, 2013
Glenlawn Collegiate honoured Gabe during its 2013 Glenlawn Collegiate Athletics Awards Banquet, inducting him into the Glenlawn Wall of Fame in the Builder category. Jonathan Wolfe, Physical Education teacher, summed up Gabe's merits for the award as he introduced Gabe and invited him to the podium:

> Take a look around... chances are, our next inductee has been at almost all of the events that you have attended... chances are Dancing Gabe Langlois was there, sharing his signature dance moves and constant energy over the last 20 years.
>
> Who is Dancing Gabe?
>
> Dancing Gabe has been a fixture on the Manitoba professional and amateur sports scene. He is "the superman" and his positive cheering and dancing have provided many fans with great experiences and lasting memories. Gabe tirelessly volunteers his time to bring his energy and spirit to as many events as possible. He dances during every music break and during intermissions works the crowd, high-fiving anyone and everyone. Dancing Gabe's signature dance moves are both original and creative...
>
> This year in particular has been special for Gabe. He recently celebrated his 50th birthday and was a recipient of the prestigious Queen's Diamond Jubilee Medal...
>
> There is no question that Dancing Gabe's commitment to spirit and positive energy has had a major contribution on sport in Manitoba. Further, his class and enthusiasm helped lay the foundation for our school spirit and cheering.
>
> It is with great honour that I welcome one of the most iconic and genuinely spirited Manitobans as a builder to the Glenlawn Wall of Fame.

CFL

CHAPTER 14

Summers in St. Vital

People rarely succeed unless they have fun in what they are doing.
—Dale Carnegie

Every summer, both before and after Gabe's years away, the Langlois family were active in a host of recreational pursuits. On weekends, they would often go to Birds Hill or Patricia Beach. Sunny Sunday outings were a favourite for Louis, who enjoyed being a kid with his kids, splashing around and throwing a football or a Frisbee.

During the week, Gabe developed a passion for swimming, spending most of his free time with his siblings at Centennial Pool.

"We lived at the pool, all of us," remembers Rick. "The lifeguards knew us, and we were there all day!"

Gabe still remembers the names of lifeguards whose work of keeping an eye on him kept them on their toes and more than deserving of their wages. Among the Langlois siblings, Gabe was the best at holding his breath under water. "He could stay under water forever," Gerry says. "His favourite trick was to hold his breath, sink down with his eyes open. I would dive down to make sure he was okay, and he would hold me down. I had to punch him in the gut so he would let go of me, otherwise I would have drowned."

Gabe loved to do the deadman float. "He would just lie in there, motionless, holding his breath," Claudette recalls. "At some point, the lifeguards would blow their whistles but Gabe didn't hear them, so they would jump in, poke him and tell him to stop it! Sometimes they would tell him to go and sit out for ten minutes."

While the Langlois kids made good use of their family pool pass, they had other adventures. Gabe first visited the Red River Exhibition during the summer of 1976, and he boasts that he has not missed the Ex since. His favourite ride continues to be the Flying Bob. “No, I never got sick,” he claims.

The summer of 1978 was particularly memorable. It was the summer of the movie Grease and the movie Foul Play—with Goldie Hawn and Chevy Chase, as Gabe accurately points out. It was the summer he jumped off the three-metre diving board and did cannonballs, and the summer of the Commonwealth Games in Edmonton, which he watched on television. Gabe is quick to recall that Canadians Graham Smith won six gold medals in swimming and Diane Jones-Konihowsky captured gold in the women’s heptathlon.

Streaking

In the summer of 1975, at age twelve, Gabe went streaking down Hull Avenue. He still laughs about it. It happened in an era when streakers—people who would run naked through a public place as a prank, a dare, or an act of protest—were appearing at sporting events, attracting plenty of media coverage. The popular 1974 song “The Streak,” by Ray Stevens, had been released in 1974 and became one of Gabe’s instant favourites, and possibly an inspiration for his spontaneous action.

When he noticed Gabe had left the house in the nude, Rick caught up to him at about the same time police officers were putting him in the cruiser. “The cops knew our family,” Rick recalls. “They liked my Dad, got along with him really well, so they looked after Gabe.”

Needless to say, they gave him a ride home that day.

Can I speak to Batman, please?

That same year, Gabe acted on one more of his cultural loves: comic books. “He loved comics from the age of four,” Angélina recalls. “He would spend hours and hours turning the pages of Marvel comics. He never ripped a single page from those magazines."

Gabe says his favourites included Superman, the Flash, and especially Batman. Gotham, Batman's home, represents a very special place for Gabe.

On that memorable day, Gabe took the phone and dialled zero for New York City, which he understood to be Gotham. After only a few rings, the long distance operator came on.

"What city please?"

"Gotham City."

After a few moments of silence, the operator's voice chimed in the earpiece.

"Can you tell me who you would like to speak to?"

"I would like to speak to Batman please," answered Gabe, in a most serious tone.

"Is everything okay?"

"Yes, I just want to speak to Batman, please," Gabe repeated impatiently.

The operator then asked to speak to one of Gabe's parents. Gabe called Angélina and handed her the phone. He watched his mom attentively during the brief exchange, wondering if she might be talking to Batman. She was laughing.

"Batman doesn't take calls," Angélina told Gabe after thanking the operator and hanging up the phone. "He's too busy."

Gabe hung his head and walked away, obviously disappointed that the caped crusader could not come to the phone.

LIONS

CHAPTER 15

Hockey, a Passion!

> The winters of my childhood were long, long seasons. We lived in three places—the school, the church and the skating rink—but our real life was on the skating rink. Real battles were won on the skating rink. Real strength appeared on the skating rink.[22]
>
> —*Roch Carrier,* The Hockey Sweater

If the Langlois siblings spent their summer months swimming, they spent the other nine months playing or watching hockey. "There were two religions in our house," Rob says "Hockey Night in Canada on Saturday nights, and going to church on Sunday mornings." Angélina and her kids attest unanimously to Louis' passion for hockey: Dad was a huge Montreal Canadiens fan.

Hockey surrounded Gabe. His siblings all played, most of them to a high calibre, and his mother and father rarely missed their children's games—which means Gabe also rarely missed a game. In the wintertime, the Langlois family practically lived at the St. Vital Arena, at Windsor Community Centre, and at Norberry Community Centre.

"Hockey was our life," says Gerry. "We played hockey in the house, in the hallway. We played hockey outside; we had rinks everywhere. Dad would teach us how to make them, and soon all the brothers learned the fine art of preparing and flooding some of the finest natural ice Winnipeg had to offer."

Rob remembers a time when his dad came to watch him play. "My Dad liked the fights but not the dirty fights. He gave me heck after a game because of a cheap shot I had dished out. You could be tough, but you had to be fair."

Claudette's hockey team. Claudette is second from right, front row. Coaches Jowett, Louis, Rick, and Mike (in back row, L-R).

Rick recalls playing for the Pee Wee AA Vics, "One Saturday, I was waiting for Dad to pick me up and take me to the rink." As every young kid did, Rick watched the clock's little hand move so slowly, painfully. When the seconds turned to minutes, and the minutes to tens of minutes, and Louis was not home yet, Angélina realized that Rick had to leave if he would make it to the game. She helped Rick put on his hockey gear, told him to put on his coat, and took him to the bus stop, stick and skates on his shoulder. "I was just in time for puck drop," says Rick. "Mr. Gaudreault, my coach, was waiting on the front steps of the arena. He laced my skates, put on my helmet, and I jumped into the action.

Claudette started playing hockey at the age of five. Mike signed her up, but since girls were not allowed on boys' teams at the time, he registered his sister as "Claude," a fitting boy's name. Without knowing it, Claudette may have started a trend for girls; today, opportunities abound for girls to play organized hockey to the highest caliber.

She remembers Mom and Dad getting excited during some of her games at St. Vital Arena. But never were they more excited than in 1975, when she skated at the Winnipeg Arena between periods—a breakaway on Joe "The Holy Goalie" Daley. As the puck hit the back of the net, the crowd erupted. It then gave Claudette a rousing ovation as she skated an unforgettable victory lap.

Jill Mathez, the first woman to be inducted in the Manitoba Hockey Hall of Fame and Claudette's teammate for many years, recalls playing hockey with Gabe's sister. "Claudette was an amazing player. She was fast and she had moves," says Jill. "Those were the days. We were trailblazing. There was nothing organized when it came to girls playing hockey back then, but we persevered."

Jill admits that the girls had a lot of fun. The two of them eventually joined the Fort Garry Angels, and later the Canadian Polish Athletic Club (CPAC) team, and finally a twenty-five-plus sponge hockey team, the Power Puffs.

Mike Langlois preferred refereeing to playing, eventually officiating in the Manitoba Junior Hockey League (MJHL). At seventeen he was named head referee for Manitoba's Junior B Hockey. He moved to the Western Hockey League (WHL) when the Winnipeg Warriors were established in Winnipeg in 1980. He would later apply for a linesman and referee job in the International Hockey League (IHL) when the Manitoba Moose moved to Winnipeg, after the Jets left for Phoenix. His work with the IHL eventually took him to San Diego, where he still resides with his family.

But for all of the family's passion for the sport, Gabe never learned to skate, let alone play hockey. Claudette tells of her attempt to introduce him to skating when he was fifteen or sixteen. "I brought Gabe once to Windsor Community Centre, along with Mike's skates. I laced his skates for him. He tried really hard to skate but he pretty much had to hold on to the boards the whole time. He didn't use a hockey stick. He didn't like it."

Nephew Ryan describes the atmosphere when the Langlois siblings and their children watch hockey on television today. "It gets really serious. There's lots of yelling, sometimes swearing, at the TV," he says. "It's Suzie, [Rob's wife] who usually has to tell us to calm down."

Scrambled eggs, anyone?

Rick and Gerry recall a time, in their Chandos Avenue home, when the weather outside was rainy, and the kids had to play indoors. Aunt Elisabeth, Louis' sister, was visiting from Quebec with her kids. The action took place early in the day.

"We all went upstairs with our sticks to a bedroom that was still empty, and started a game," Gerry remembers. "But we got bored with the usual game, and Mike had the bright idea to take a dozen eggs from the refrigerator, while nobody was watching." It seemed like a good idea at the time. What harm could come from playing indoor hockey? With raw eggs!

At first the boys really got into it, shooting with abandon. Splat! First on the walls, but then it seemed much more fun to shoot at someone; Claudette maybe. Once the eggs were all broken, the boys sat down and admired their handy work. Things got really quiet.

They heard their father shouting downstairs. "Angèle! It's pretty quiet up there. Why don't you go up and see what the boys are up to." Angélina complied, and Louis soon followed her.

They both stood in the doorway, speechless. Just when the kids thought they were in for a stiff scolding, much to their surprise, Louis grabbed a stick and Angélina a broom, and joined in for one more rush on the slippery floor.

Gabe's first Jets game

Monday, May 22, 1978

Gabe's first Jets game at the old Winnipeg Arena is etched in his memory. "Mike took me to see the WHA Jets play. On that night, they defeated the New England Whalers 5–3 to win their second of three consecutive AVCO Cups, sweeping the Whalers in four straight." The Jets would repeat the feat the following year, just before the World Hockey Association was swallowed up by the National Hockey League. That game, in May 1978, turned out to be Anders Hedberg and Ulf

Nilsson's last game as Winnipeg Jets. They were traded to the New York Rangers.

Gabe also remembers Winnipeg's last AVCO Cup, "They defeated the Oilers on May 20, 1979, by a score of 7–3 at the Winnipeg Arena."

Gabe did not dance that night, but he cheered for his home team, as he would often do in years to come. "The crowd went wild," he says. "I remember Al Shaver [Canadian Hall of Fame broadcaster who was the Voice of the Minnesota North Stars at the time] said: 'Down goes Jibberville.'"

It would be three years before Gabe would see an NHL game in Winnipeg. "My first NHL Jets 1.0 game was in 1983, when the Jets played the St. Louis Blues, early in the season."

WINNIPEG
JETS

CHAPTER 16

Part of the Team, Part of the Family

> An autistic person's fixations can be their way to achieve some social life and friends.
>
> —*Temple Grandin, in* Thinking in Pictures

Asked how he developed his passion for dancing, Gabe explains, "I saw Michael Jackson do the moonwalk during the Motown 25th Anniversary back in 1983. I was amazed! That was it! I've been trying to perfect that move ever since."

But his mom joins the conversation and reveals a little secret.

"I think he got his start with the Jolly Jumper," she ventures. "Gabe would dance in the Jolly Jumper and try to keep up with the rest of his siblings. He liked music so much. Later on I bought him a cassette player and he always took good care of it, listened to it for countless hours."

Fascinated with dancing, passionate, maybe even a little obsessed, Gabe has never stopped dancing since.

There is no denying that for Gabe, dancing has been at the heart of his social life.

"Dancing Gabe" is now official

Monday, January 21, 1991

Gabe had been strutting his stuff for almost eight years, unofficially, at Bombers and Jets games. Many had referred to him as Dancing Gabe during that time. Unofficially, that is. Then came the unforgettable night in Gabe's life, a few days before he turned twenty-eight.

That night, Mike and Gabe took the bus to the Winnipeg Arena, as they had many times before. It was cold, darn cold, and windy, not uncommon for a Winnipeg winter night.

"The Jets defeated the Minnesota North Stars by a score of 2–0," Gabe remembers with his usual precision.

Early in the game, as Gabe sat beside his brother in the southwest corner of the lower bowl, a gentleman carrying a special gift approached him. Gabe recognized Mike O'Hearn, the Jets' director of public relations at the time.

At previous games Mike had watched Gabe from high in the team's press box. He liked what he saw and thought it would only be fitting for the team to recognize Gabe's energy and passion. "I said to Lori (Summers), my co-worker, I'm going to meet him and get him a jersey. He's a really good guy for the team. He inspires people and generates enthusiasm in the crowd."

Mike had made his way to the arena bowl, on a previous night, and caught up to Gabe. He was immediately impressed by the bespectacled young man full of dancing energy. Mike introduced himself, asked Gabe for his name, and chatted with him for a few minutes. Tonight, he had come with a special gift.

With many fans watching the scene, Mike shook Gabe's hand and handed him a brand new Jets jersey. Gabe recognized the Jets logo on the front and beamed with pride, speechless. But then Mike turned the jersey to display the back.

"Gabe, I think it's time we made it official. You are now 'Dancing Gabe', officially!"

A star was born...

"The fans around him absolutely loved it," Mike recalls. "They were charged up seeing him put on the jersey. I think it put an exclamation mark on Gabe. I've been a huge fan of his ever since."

Mike doesn't take credit for Gabe's success. "All I wanted to do was recognize him," says the former executive, who moved to Phoenix with

"Gabe has a rare ability—life is better knowing that Gabe's around. At Jets games, with my Dad, when Gabe came by, you knew everything was ok."
—*Ace Burpee, Winnipeg media personality (Virgin Radio) and passionate ambassador for the City of Winnipeg*

the Jets back in 1996. "We made sure he could get at the games; he never looked for donations, just [wanted to be] a classy fan. He would be at every autograph signing session, and the team community events."

Mike reminisces about the emotionally difficult months leading to the sale and the eventual move of the Jets to Phoenix. "It was very difficult to leave. Winnipeg had become home for me and my family," Mike says. He agrees with the Langlois family that the team's departure was one of the most difficult times for Gabe as well.

"Everybody was very aware of Gabe during that last year. He summed up the passion of Winnipeg for the team. He epitomized the Jets fan. He became the essence of Winnipeg. The players recognized Gabe: they saw him. Win or lose, he was a fan!"

The discussion reverts to Gabe, his boundless energy and his ability to dance the crowd into a frenzy. "Yeah, some people would chuckle and laugh, but you know, he's the real deal. Gabe represented the fan emotion, their importance and their connection with the team."

Asked if he was aware of Gabe's intellectual disability, Mike admits, "I recognized it but I never saw it that way. He is a true success."

Wise Guys

Angélina tells of the relationship between the Langlois family and former Winnipeg Jet Perry Miller, whom she regarded almost as one of her own children. Perry played with the Jets from 1974 to 1976, and then with the Detroit Red Wings from 1976 to 1981. Moving back to Winnipeg in 1993, he took on the job of general manager of Norma Jean's, a popular downtown nightclub. A few years later, Perry joined a group of local businessmen and launched Wise Guys, a hopping sports bar and Winnipeg institution, located in Winnipeg's historic Exchange District from 1993 to 2002, with a second location at the University of Manitoba campus until it closed in 2010.

A 2011 *Toronto Sun* article quotes Perry, saying, "We built personal relationships with quite a few of the Winnipeg Jets players that used to come down there—Keith Tkachuk and Teemu (Selanne) and Teppo (Numminen). You had your favourites, but also the visiting teams used to come in there too."

It was through Gabe's brother Mike that Perry first got to know the Langlois family. "I was friends with Mike," he explains. "We skated at lunch time at St. Vital Arena with a bunch of real estate guys."

"The Old Timers team kept an enviable road schedule," Perry says. "I know Mike went with them to Europe one year. It's how I first became acquainted with Dancing Gabe and his family. Gabe would come right in at Wise Guys. He was everyone's friend. The doormen would take him under their wings and keep an eye on him, ensure he was safe and having a good time."

Kate Gameiro, a former Wise Guys events director, adds colour to Perry's stories. "We knew a little bit about Gabe. He just started showing up at the back door—the VIP entrance. I think he was only ever asked for his pass once, the first time," Kate recalls, laughing. "Gabe was never in anybody's way. He became part of the place, part of the family."

Bob Sokalski, one of Wise Guys' owners, summarizes a typical Wise Guys game night back in the day, when Gabe would have been in his early thirties. "When Gabe was in the house, it was infectious. At 4:30 p.m., we would start the BBQ and Gabe would bring cheer to the room. When it was time to catch the bus [to a game], Gabe was the first on, and the first off. Then he's off to work, to do his thing. And at the end of the night, when we all get back on the bus, Gabe feeds off the energy of the other fans."

If you ask Gabe what mode of transportation he preferred, undoubtedly he would say, "The bus!" The famous Wise Guys bus was a familiar sight and a first-rate method of transportation from the bar to the games and back. Gabe's usual seat on the bus was at the front. According to Perry, "Gabe always goes to the front of the line, that's the norm, but he thinks nothing of it."

Kate Gameiro states a truth that would only become more obvious as Dancing Gabe's fame grew, "From a marketing perspective, Dancing Gabe is gold!" She recalls a photograph that hung on the wall at Wise Guys, a keepsake from an event that highlighted Gabe's popularity. "It was a grainy photo of the late Kevin Walters—a tower of strength in Winnipeg's arts and entertainment community, who left us much too soon—imitating Dancing Gabe during the Ultimate Pub Crawl. And, you know, everybody in the place knew exactly who he was imitating!"

Kate tells of the time when Perry approached the Blue Bombers management, back in 1996, to discuss the possibility of allowing Gabe at games for free. The idea did not generate much enthusiasm at the time. Undeterred, Perry brought his idea to the other Wise Guys partners, and eventually Wise Guys purchased season's tickets to the Blue Bombers, allowing Dancing Gabe to attend every game at no cost, for a number of years. Wise Guys also gave Gabe personalized jerseys, with "Dancing Gabe" on the back and the Wise Guys logo on the front. Nobody seemed to mind, least of all Dancing Gabe. Warren's Corner Sports had done something similar for Gabe a few years earlier, giving him a number of tickets to Jets and Bombers games, and a sweater with the store's name and Dancing Gabe's name on the back.

Perry even invited Gabe and his mom to attend fundraising dinners and other Wise Guys-organized events. On one occasion, he invited Gabe and Angélina to sit at the Wise Guys table, along with Moose forward Greg Pankiewicz, CKY television's senior news anchor Barbara-Lee Edwards, and Bob Sokalski and his wife Barb. The evening included limousine service for Gabe and Angélina.

But Perry is quick to clarify: "Gabe never asked for anything. He just wanted to be a part of it. Gabe is the biggest ambassador of sports in Winnipeg. There's no reason he should have had to pay for tickets, especially when he spends most of his time up and dancing."

More important than the mutually beneficial relationship between Wise Guys and Dancing Gabe, however, was the personal relationship between Perry and Gabe that still endures after more than twenty years.

Asked what Dancing Gabe means to Winnipeg, Perry is quick to reply. "If Gabe is there, you know it's a worthwhile event. Gabe played a role in trying to keep the Jets here. Heck, when the Jets announced their return, there were three people in front at the events: the Premier, the Mayor, and Dancing Gabe!"

"I think Gabe lives for the moment," notes Kate. "He is appreciative of everyone, in his own way, and he's always happy." Kate can't resist revealing Gabe's playful side. "On game night, he'd chat up the pretty girls and they would seek him out too! He can be a big flirt, you know."

Bob Sokalski adds his own perspective and colour: "Gabe is not just a fan, he's a fanatic—in a good way—about sports, passionate. That's his full time job! For every team, even the college and minor teams. I think Gabe endeared himself to a whole new audience when he started attending [University of Manitoba] Bison and [University of Winnipeg] Wesmen games. Gabe is the heart and soul of the hometown crowd at any game and any sport. The remarkable thing about Gabe—one of them—is that he is absolutely untainted by any negativity. He is there with the same energy, win or lose, rain or shine. He's poignant—but he's not a team mascot."

Some of Gabe's biggest fans are well aware of what Wise Guys did for him. Someone unrelated to Wise Guys even suggested that the corporate support—putting the Wise Guys name on his jerseys, and buying him tickets to games—likely gave Dancing Gabe a purpose, a real opportunity to do his thing.

SAVE THE JETS
RAP BOOK
DE COUPURES
RECORD ROOKIE!
SELANNE SHATTERS BOSSY'S STANDARD

CHAPTER 17

Rooting for the Moose and the Jets

Gabe means a lot to us, the Moose or the Jets, because he accepted us for what we are, win or lose, NHL or AHL. I have a deep appreciation for Gabe's real passion; he is a pure fan, unquestionably. Truly. He's always there!

—Mark Chipman, Executive Chairman of the Board of True North Sports & Entertainment Limited and Winnipeg Jets Hockey Club

In the months preceding the Jets' final decision to leave Winnipeg in May 1995, fans and organizations deployed tremendous efforts to raise funds and keep them in Manitoba. During those days, Gabe worked tirelessly at the CJOB radio station, day and night, receiving and picking up donations from fans.

Angélina remembers that "Gabe was gone every day, all day. He would come home totally exhausted."

He attended a number of "Save the Jets" rallies at Portage and Main, and spent time at The Forks alongside Winnipeg sports and entertainment personalities, promoting the cause, fundraising, and signing autographs. After the decision, Gabe also took part in a Wise Guys pub crawl, to help fans deal with the departure of the Jets. The bar even created a T-shirt for the occasion, with its logo proclaiming, "Last one to leave, turn out the lights!"

Rick Langlois puts the announcement of the Jets departure in perspective, an especially painful time for Gabe. "Gabe was very sad when

Dad passed away [in 1983] and he was out of sorts for a long time. But he didn't show as much emotion back then as he did when the Jets left. He was very emotional and cried for long hours. He just couldn't get over it."

The day after the Jets were sold, Gabe called his brother. "Rick, I want to go for a beer! Please," is all Gabe said on the phone. A strange request because for all Rick knew, Gabe did not drink beer; he had never seen him drink. But he agreed, and shortly after picked him up at home.

At Big Guy's Ranch & Saloon, Gabe drank three beers that night, and could not stop talking about the Jets leaving. He may have been a little drunk, nobody knows for sure. But he was genuinely hurt.

Mike O'Hearn, former Jets' director of public relations, remembers those days as if it was yesterday. "We [the team] were rooting for the folks who tried to save the Jets and keep them in Winnipeg. The last game in Winnipeg tugged at our heartstrings. The people in Winnipeg make the difference. They are tremendous fans and the sense of community is still absolutely overwhelming."

This remains an emotional topic for him. On a brighter note, he explains, "It's somewhat ironic how things have turned around. I think the return of the Jets has improved the NHL, all around."

The NHL is big business. Mike sums it up quite accurately. "Ultimately, the events are a credit to the economy, to the Winnipeg fans, and to some very committed owners, like Mark Chipman."

Once the pain of losing the Jets subsided, Gabe quickly adopted the Manitoba Moose as his new team. He would always keep a soft spot for the Jets, and a secret hope that one day they would return. However, the show had to go on; life had to continue after the Jets.

With the smaller, younger crowd at Moose games, Gabe developed a renewed energy and a few new moves. Unwittingly, he would compete for the crowd's attention alongside his good buddy, Mick E. Moose, the Moose's antlered mascot.

Ryan, Gabe's nephew remembers it well, "There were were always kids—so many minor hockey teams went to Moose games all the time—following Mick E. Moose. But I think there were more kids following Gabe!"

Scott Arniel

Scott Arniel knows a thing or two about Dancing Gabe. After all, Scott played with both the Winnipeg Jets and Manitoba Moose. He captained the Moose, was traded, and eventually returned as the team's head coach.

"I remember seeing him at Safeway on Grant Avenue. Gabe was bagging groceries. I approached him and said 'Hey, Dancing Gabe! How are you?' but Gabe stopped me, and very seriously, almost whispering, he said 'No, no, Scott. Here, I'm not Dancing Gabe. Only Gabe.'" (At the time, Gabe was taking a crack at a regular eight-to-four job arranged by his caseworker. He would eventually return to his work at the YMCA).

"You could always tell where Gabe was in the building," Scott remembers of his days at the MTS Centre. "There was a ripple that followed him, a wave of kids dancing, imitating him. Even the players would be looking for him during commercial time-outs, although they weren't supposed to."

Gabe never got tired of it. On the concourse, he would kneel down as the line of little players paraded by, leaving his hand outstretched as high as the kids could reach, their small hands making contact with Gabe's. Some would even ask Gabe for an autograph, and then run proudly back to their seats, exhilarated.

A key challenge for professional sports teams is to find activities to entertain fans during stoppages in play and down time. But Dancing Gabe provided an easy solution to this problem. "He is almost an extension of the staff and the entertainment crew," says Scott. "He is also very respectful of everyone and of the fact that they have a job to do. He's part of the landscape. He's always welcome, anywhere." Scott adds that the kind of respect Gabe demonstrates earns him the same respect from the teams' owners and players.

When reminiscing about the Moose days, Gabe often tells a funny story—a funny story that Scott is quite familiar with—about helping the Moose players' wives organize the annual carnival. When asked for his perspective on the story, Scott holds up his hand, in a "stop" motion, laughing. "There's no truth to that rumour." The rumour? That Scott may have become a little suspicious of all the phone calls between Lia (Scott's wife) and Gabe, and that Scott might have told Gabe, in jest, that the calling would have to stop. Scott bursts out laughing.

"Gabe was very helpful, and persistent," Scott says. "I think one thing that sets Gabe apart, and a reason why people appreciate him, is that he's not in your face. He's actually a little shy."

It's hard to believe that anyone would use the word *shy* in the same sentence as 'Dancing Gabe.' But it is accurate. Despite all appearances of friendliness and engagement, Gabe is a very reserved person.

In 1997, Gabe was named honorary team captain of the Moose. The team and FastSigns even produced the *Top 5 Dancing Gabe Moves* video, immortalizing Gabe's legendary moves. Gabe derived great pride from the video. "I always wanted to do the Moonwalk like Michael Jackson. And now, I had my own moves. That was great!" says Gabe.

Legend has it that Dancing Gabe was the first fan to set foot in the MTS Centre when the new facility opened on November 16, 2004.

Gabe was given his own Moose jersey and a media pass for the first Moose game at the Centre. That evening, he received his share of cheers whenever he showed up on the big screen, dancing to the music. "The fans love to see him. He's part of the games and part of the family," says Kyle Balharry, the Senior Director of Game Production & Broadcast Services for True North Sports & Entertainment.

"It's an awesome arena," Gabe says. "The restaurants, the lounge, Moxie's, the seating, the sound, the scoreboard. And seating is way more comfortable than the old Winnipeg Arena."

The one-minute FastSign video features the song "Safety Dance," by the Canadian band Men Without Hats. A youthful looking Gabe, blond highlights in his hair, dressed in a Moose home jersey and beige pants, performs moves called Caped Crusader, Stair Master, Fist of Fury, Dual Air Guitar, and finally, the Tornado.

Dancing Gabe has slowed down somewhat since the days of the video but fans still enjoy watching him pump his fist to the beat, spin around and strum out a few chords on his air guitar. Nobody does it better.

Jets return!

The return of the Jets and the NHL to Winnipeg in 2011 was the most important sporting event to hit the city since the Pan American Games in 1999. The event generated a huge crescendo of fan excitement leading up to the regular season games that fall—an excitement that reached new heights in 2015 as the Jets made the playoffs.

> "You want popularity? Cults would kill to have the following he has. Consider the fans who gathered at the intersection of Portage and Main in Winnipeg to celebrate the return of the NHL in May 2011. When Langlois joined the throng, the chants of "Go, Jets, Go!" were quickly replaced by "Gabe, Gabe, Gabe!" and he was mobbed for pictures and high fives."
>
> —*Geoff Kirbyson,* Winnipeg Free Press *reporter,* The Hockey News—The Fan Issue, *November 24th, 2014*

Along with the team's return came renewed energy and enthusiasm from Dancing Gabe. As a River City Sports blog put it, "Besides the Prime Minister, Tkachuk and Hawerchuk, Kreviazuk and (Jim) Cuddy, and even Canadian baseball stars Corey Koskie and Justin Morneau, Dancing Gabe was in the house. If Dancing Gabe has a place to strut his stuff then all is right with the world."

Dancing Gabe could be seen in newspaper articles, in news reports, and online. He showed up at the many official events commemorating the return of the team. One *Winnipeg Free Press* reporter caught up with Gabe, "the most famously mobile Jets fan of all," at Portage and Main, after police shut down festivities at The Forks. According to the news article, Gabe shouted, "I'm ready to dance. It's going to be the greatest day in Winnipeg sports history."

Gabe also earned a mention in Jonathon Gatehouse's account of the Jets' home opener in his book, *The Instigator: How Gary Bettman Remade the League and Changed the Game Forever*:

> "Dancing Gabe" Langlois, a simple soul who found notoriety jiving in the stands of the old Winnipeg Arena as a chubby, curly-haired youth, is on hand with his new team gear, older, greyer, and still gyrating for all he's worth. The nostalgia is palpable, but there's something more underpinning the party: relief. "Fifteen years ago, it was like someone stuck a fist between your ribs and pulled your heart out," says Sam Katz, Winnipeg's current mayor.
>
> What was once lost has been found. And the city—and the country—is celebrating. Proof, finally, that bigger isn't necessarily better. That passion can count for more than dollars. That the game we claim still belongs to us. A win, even if it is by default.

Let the games begin

Kevin Klein, then CEO and publisher at the *Winnipeg Sun*, recalls the fuss about Gabe possibly not getting tickets to the new edition of the Jets: "Editors in Winnipeg were shocked, upset even, and had reporters digging around to confirm that the rumour was false. That's a true sign of how much people care for Gabe in this city."

Geoff Kirbyson, *Winnipeg Free Press* reporter, similarly reported that the team wasn't going to leave Gabe out in the cold. He quoted Jets spokesman Scott Brown as saying, "He's been a loyal supporter of the Jets brand. We're supportive of people who have supported us."

At the Jets return party at Portage and Main, Kevin Klein remembers, "We didn't have to tell reporters to get a picture of Dancing Gabe: he was on the front page the next morning! There was never an argument about the front page story."

Mark Chipman's reflections

In his usual calm and thoughtful demeanour, Mark Chipman talks about a more personal aspect of his relationship with Gabe. "The first time I got a Christmas card from Gabe, I was really touched. That was probably the first year of the Moose. And the tradition has continued ever since, every year. You know, he hand-delivers the cards," he says.

Everyone on Gabe's Christmas card list admits that the cards are very special to him or her, but it is the very way Gabe delivers them—by bus!—that most touches each of them. A genuine display of affection and appreciation, in a way only Dancing Gabe can.

When asked about the essentials of Dancing Gabe, Mark needs only a few seconds to ponder the question. "Gabe represents a lot of people. We have lots of fans, not all like him, but fans nonetheless. He believes in the City, no matter what happens."

A pause. Mark then delivers his final punch. "Gabe's always there for you. You can count on him. We're in a hard business; he makes it better."

That's quite an endorsement from the man who, along with fellow businessmen, brought the Moose to Winnipeg after the Jets' departure so the city could continue to enjoy professional hockey—and who, fifteen years later, through sheer dedication and perseverance, would bring the Jets back.

"Kudos to the teams for making sure he has a place. Especially to Mark Chipman to recognize Gabe's important birthday. Most importantly, he recognized him as a person, as a human being."

—Kevin Klein, President and CEO of MyToba.ca

Angélina never hesitates to express her gratitude for Mark.

"Mister Chipman is such a nice man. He has been really good to Gabe and to our entire family. We owe him much."

Gabe nods his head in agreement and adds, "That's true! I like Mark."

CHAPTER 18

Game Day with the Jets

Essentially, Gabe has achieved a legendary status.

—Kyle Balharry, the Senior Director of Game Production & Broadcast Services for True North Sports & Entertainment

Sunday, November 23, 2014

It's Game Day! The Jets are playing the St. Louis Blues this afternoon.

It is a grey, very grey morning. The drizzle melts the thin layer of snow that fell the night before, revealing grass the colour of peanut butter cookies. The streets have not yet received their usual sprinkling of sand and other abrasive materials that invariably will turn everything to brown. Life on the Prairies.

And yet there is excitement in the air, because the Jets are playing a home game. The city is abuzz. So is Dancing Gabe. Like most Winnipeg sports fans, he cares about the team's record, but his dedication, his love of the game, and his support for the team never waver, regardless of how they perform.

Claudette offers to drive Gabe and me to the game today, and he accepts. Keeta, the family's Husky-Shepherd cross, stares out the living room window, unimpressed, as if to say "You are going out in this mess?" Gabe gives Keeta a hug, and proceeds out the door—carefully, because the drizzle is still falling and everything is now covered with a shiny coat of ice.

"Wow! Look at all this traffic," remarks Claudette as she makes her way onto St. Mary's Road. The wipers beat a frantic rhythm, doing

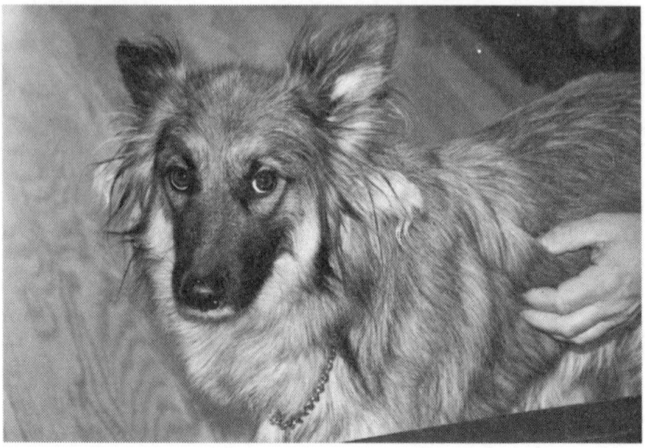

Keeta

their best to keep the drizzle from freezing on the windshield. From the Norwood Bridge, only a diffuse outline of downtown's tallest buildings is visible; they seem to float in an eerie grey haze, shrouded by the thickening fog. The sanding crews have been out.

The drizzle has turned to a steady rain by the time we arrive at the corner of Graham and Hargrave, across from the MTS Centre. Stepping out of the car requires vigilance and something to hang on to, or maybe a pair of studded boots. Gabe does a strange little dance as he steps to the sidewalk and walks briskly to the media entrance.

The attendant greets Gabe with a warm hug and bright smile, inquiring about his whereabouts since the last game. They chat briefly. Once through the doors, Gabe quickly disappears.

By the time I get my pass and proceed through the door. Gabe is nowhere to be seen; I have lost him, again! One of the ushers, whose name tag says Tony, points to the concession behind him. "Gabe always gets his popcorn there," he tells me. Then he points to a few metal folding chairs. "And he always sits here to eat his popcorn, and watch the pre-game skate."

Just as Tony predicted, Gabe arrives a few minutes later carrying a bag of popcorn.

Fans of all ages file in and the place begins to buzz. Many notice Gabe and walk over to give him a hi-five. A mom taps her young son on the shoulder, gently, and points toward Dancing Gabe. The youngster hurries over to Gabe for a fist pump and a hi-five. He returns with a bounce in his step and a smile from ear to ear. The scene will play itself out at least a hundred times by the time the teams take to the ice. Gabe is everybody's fan.

With every minute, the noise level rises. More people file in, some wandering, others clearly seeking a destination, many greeting friends. Talking, chatting, smiling, laughing... and lots of noise. It's about noise. Make some noise.

Loud music and bright lights come on, and soon the teams take to the ice for the pre-game skate. The players perform their pre-game routines. Lots of pucks flying. Fans lined up against the glass, trying to get the players' attention.

"These are the best seats in the house for the pre-game skate," Gabe says, indicating the metal folding chairs. The energy level in the MTS Centre cranks up yet another notch on a scale that seems to have no limit.

His popcorn bag discarded, Gabe begins his own pre-game routine, stretching and warming up. Then he leaves his seat for a few minutes. He walks over to Moxie's Grill & Bar and peeks at the televisions through the window, trying to determine the outcome of the CFL's Eastern Final between Montreal and Hamilton. It appears the Tiger Cats have come out on top, which Gabe says, "will make for an interesting Grey Cup."

Finally, the teams return to the ice and everyone stands for the "Star-Spangled Banner" and "O Canada." The roar of an F-18 jet fighter, barely audible over the cheers from the crowd, resonates from every corner and announces the time to play hockey. It's time for Dancing Gabe to get to work.

Around the lower bowl, from section to section, he patiently awaits a stoppage in play, then proceeds to the landing that separates the 100s from the 200s, grooves to the music and the encouragement of the fans, and cheers people on. Many extend a hand for a hi-five or a fist-pump as he walks by; others ready their cell phone cameras for a quick

Gabe and Mark Chipman

photo. When play resumes, Gabe moves to the top of the stairway and exchanges a few words with event staff, who all seem to agree when it comes to Dancing Gabe, "He's got so much energy! And he always remembers our names! How does he do it?"

At 10:56 of the first period the Jets score their first goal. The arena erupts in celebration—the horn, the lights, the players, and the fans. The noise is simply deafening. Everybody is standing. Those near Gabe reach out to give him a hi-five. His face lights up.

Gabe and I schedule our intermission rendezvous. Gabe's instruction are crystal clear: "By the elevator, five minutes before the end of the first period."

He is at the post, on time. With anticipation (for me, the rookie; probably not so much for Gabe, the pro), the elevator lifts us to the fifth floor and the press gallery.

We emerge on the fifth floor and make it through a brief security check. Our vantage point high above the action provides an awesome view of the game that the fans don't see. We can see the entire ice surface surrounded by the sold-out crowd, along with a close-up view of the building's structure. Gabe leans on the railing and watches the end of the period.

The horn at the end of the period causes a surprising chain reaction on the fifth floor. The hallway, relatively quiet a second ago, instantly buzzes with activity, people emerging from their offices to refresh their coffee, visit the bathroom, or simply stretch their legs.

At the convent in Notre-Dame-de-Lourdes, circa 1946. **Mlle Angélina Dumas**, *Sr Marie-Madeleine, Mlle Clémence, Mère Maitresse, Mlle Marie-Ange,* **Sr Marie-Augustine (Georgette Pantel)**, *Sr Agnes.*

Langlois Family, 1969. Clockwise from top left: Claudette, Angélina, Louis, Gabe, Rob, Gerry, Rick, and Mike.

The Langlois siblings, 1975. Clockwise from top left: Gabe, Mike, Rick, Rob, Claudette, and Gerry.

The house on the Boissy farm.

The honey-bucket or the outhouse.

What remains today of the chicken brooder ...

... and the barn.

Louis Langlois having breakfast, circa 1981.

Gabe's graduation picture, June 1981.

Gabe gets ready for the University of Manitoba Half-Marathon, 1987.

Gabe and Santa, circa 1995.

Gabe with niece Angela and nephew Ryan.

Gabe bowling in style and colour.

Gabe's Tuesday Night 5-Pin Bowling team. (L-R) Ron, Chris, Gabe, Gerry.

The Hot Shots. Gabe's Monday Night 10-Pin Bowling team. (L-R) Gabe, Bud, Natalie, and Al.

Gabe and Premier Gary Doer at YMCA Event in March 2007.

The Bouncer for the kids at Winnipeg's South-end YMCA.

Gabe goes for his daily 5-mile run at the YMCA, December 2014.

Mason Juras and Gabe: The Selfie.

MAIN STREET
MTS
Canada
Canada
7693
Goldeyes
1

Goldeyes
1

NCING GABE
91
91
FLIGHT
SQUADRON

Dancing Gabe meets Prime Minister Harper during the Jets playoff game, April 22, 2015. Photo by Jeff Miller. Reproduced with permission from 100 Acre Woods Photography, Winnipeg, MB.

Gabe at Dancing With Celebrities 2010, with Anahid Babaian (L) and Stephanie Blandford (R). Photo by Richard Marquez, Where to Look Photography. Reproduced with permission from the Society for Manitobans with Disabilities.

Mike, Rick, and Gabe at San Diego Zoo Safari Park in 2003.

Gabe and Angélina, in 1997.

(L-R) Rick, Mike, Gabe, Angélina, and Claudette on Hull Avenue, in July 2006.

(L-R) Ryan, Claudette, Angélina, Gabe, and Mike, August 2014.

Angélina and Gabe checking out his scrapbook collection.

Gabe proudly displays his jersey collection.

Three generations. Clockwise from left rear: Rick, Mike, Gabe, Rob, Gerry, Chanté, Claudette, Angélina, and Ryan, August 2013.

Gabe carrying the 1999 Pan Am Games torch on the streets of Winnipeg. Photo by Joe Bryksa. Reproduced with permission from the Winnipeg Free Press.

Mark Chipman is the first person to greet us. He exchanges a few words with Gabe and poses for a few pictures. Gabe makes his way deeper into the row of offices overlooking the ice. He points to the TSN 1290 booth where we find Paul Edmonds, wrapping up the period's broadcast.

The who's who of Winnipeg's sports media files by Gabe, cheerfully salute him and shake his hand. Gabe always responds with a warm smile, genuinely happy to see everyone. Gabe greets Joe Pascucci, Shawn Churchill, Scott Taylor, Mitch Peacock, and Tim Campbell. Darren Pang, former NHL goaltender and now Rogers Sportsnet's commentator, comes over and shakes Gabe's hand. We also meet with Paul Edmonds, as arranged, who makes time for a quick chat and a few pictures. But the time to go is soon upon us. Gabe retraces his steps to the elevator, hi-fiving many more on the way.

As we descend in the surreal silence of the elevator, I reflect on what a well-oiled machine the Jets organization is. The coordination and the effectiveness of the hundreds of staff and volunteers are evident all around. Customer service people are everywhere, attentive to fans' needs and eager to help, with a smile. Supervisors ensure vendors are well stocked and positioned, and all staff have the information they need. As it is with the Bombers and the Goldeyes, ensuring a premium fan experience constitutes the focus of the entire organization.

Gabe and Paul Edmonds

The way home

When we exit the MTS Centre, the temperature has plunged to –8 C with a stiff north-northwest wind of 42 kilometers an hour. Here I am, teeth chattering on Portage Avenue, waiting for our number 14 bus. As usual, however, Gabe is dressed for the elements. I should have brought a toque!

As I shiver myself into oblivion, Gabe calmly walks over to the large Moxie's window where he can now see the score of the CFL's Western Final. He reports back to me, solemnly: "Calgary 43, Edmonton 18, Dan."

I nod, no, I tremble. And all I can think about is "Someone will have to push me onto the bus if it doesn't show up soon."

Despite Winnipeg's 4–2 loss, the crowd appears upbeat. Fans walk by, recognize Gabe, wave, get closer and shake his hand. A couple asks for a selfie with him, which they take hastily, thanking him profusely before retreating quickly to the comfort of the bus shelter.

"Here comes our bus!" announces Gabe. I know he is right. He can see the number on the bus from a mile away. The bus comes to a stop and Gabe is at the door, first, as usual. I fear having to pull change out of my pockets, which will require me taking my gloved hands off my frozen ears, and they might just fall off. But I do it regardless.

Under the friendly gaze of the driver, I eventually get the right amount in the machine and make my way toward the back of the bus, where Gabe signals to me, tapping the seat to his right.

I flop onto the seat beside the big man, thankful for the heat that fills the bus. Soon, my body recognizes this new feeling—it is heat!—and I stop shivering. When that happens, I immediately start sweating.

On the way home, Gabe seems more talkative than usual. Typically, I am the one to ask the questions, and he provides only brief answers—a man of few words. But today, he initiates the conversation.

I learn that he goes to the four o'clock mass on Christmas Eve. "After church, everyone comes over to celebrate, except for Mike [who lives in San Diego]. He usually only visits during the summer."

I learn that Christmas is Gabe's favourite time of the year. He loves buying presents.

"What else do you do at this time of year?"

"I was a costumed elf in the Santa Claus Parade last week. Was it ever cold! But if you dress warm, it's not a problem."

Later I ask him, point blank, how many games he has attended in his life.

Gabe shrugs his shoulders and stares at me. We do the math together, which makes the ride seem to just fly by.

We figure that he has attended almost 1,000 hockey games since 1991, 300 Blue Bombers games since 1984, and 900 Goldeyes games, since 1994. On top of these, add the many university sports contests and amateur games he has attended.

"Wow! That is a lot of dancing Gabe! A lot of steps."

Gabe grins broadly and gives a thumbs-up. "Yeah!" is all he needs to say.

I am still cold as we emerge from the toasty bus—and sad to see the evening come to an end. I take my leave and find my truck. Brrrrr.

I scrape hard to clear the windows and eventually I drive away safely, frowning. Brrrrr. I doubt we will see freezing drizzle for a few months. Winter is here.

GABE'S DANCING BY THE NUMBERS—HOCKEY

Gabe attended a total of 540 home games (345 Moose, 195 Jets) at the old Winnipeg Arena. With its lower bowl's 35 sections and stairways, Gabe covered approximately 7,488 steps per game, for a total of 4,043,520 steps at the old Winnipeg Arena. At the MTS Centre, by the end of the season (including playoffs), Gabe attended a total of 487 games (327 Moose, 160 Jets games—he only missed one). With its lower bowl's 27 sections and stairways, Gabe covered approximately 3,672 steps per game, for a total of 1,788,264 steps at MTS Centre.

Gabe danced at his 1,000th professional hockey game in Winnipeg on December 20, 2014! For those counting, that means well over 5.8 million steps—the equivalent of walking from Vancouver to Halifax—just at hockey games! That's a lot of stepping plus a whole lotta shaking goin' on... But who is counting?

The Langlois family in 1975. (L-R) Back row: Mike, Rick, Gabe, Rob, Gerry.
Front row: Claudette, Louis, Angélina

BREAK

Louis and Angélina, Raising a Family

"Angélina, she is the rock. Her family is a testimonial to her strength, her perseverance and her love. She was the one who held the reins. She did quite a job."

—Michel Langlois, Dancing Gabe's uncle

"Dad always said what was on his mind, and somehow, it always came out funny. He was only five foot eight, but he was afraid of nobody."

—Rob Langlois

Louis-Joseph Langlois, born on March 10, 1935 to Zénon and Antonine, grew up on his father's 375-acre dairy farm in Ste. Flavie, a small town adjacent to Mont-Joli on the south shore of the St. Lawrence River. Michel, Louis' youngest brother, admits to being very close to Louis (who dropped the use of "Joseph" at a very young age). "Louis always looked out for me," he says.

Louis Langlois (who passed away in 1983) was the descendant of a family of hard-working settlers from France, the first of whom, Noël Langlois, had arrived in *Nouvelle France* more than 270 years before. Noël would settle in Beauport (Québec) on three hundred acres along the St. Lawrence River, including a seeded acre of land, given to him, along with a barrel of flour. Along with the land, Noël signs a contract with *la Compagnie de la Nouvelle-France* (the Company of New

France) to deliver 500 hay bales—now a farmer. Two years later, he would contract to supply two hundred boards measuring ten feet long, ten inches wide and an inch thick—now a carpenter.[23]

In 1683, to avoid quarrels among his children, he asks the notary-public to officially divide his land among them (that practice was not followed by Louis' father, unfortunately), a process that would last the better part of the following year. A year later, on July 14, 1684, he passes at the age of seventy-nine, apparently the oldest citizen of the country at the time.

Around the time when Angélina left the convent to resume life at home in Winnipeg (see First Break, page 68), Louis Langlois was celebrating his eighteenth birthday in in Ste. Flavie, Québec. But he had been a man for several years already; so it was when you lived on your father's dairy farm, far away from any city.

Michel recalls life on the Langlois farm, the way he and his siblings experienced it. "When Dad bought the farm, only one hundred acres were farmable; he had to clear another two hundred—he used eight horses to do that. He was strong like a bear with hands the size of shovels, a hardworking man. We had fifty wooded acres for firewood. The rest was for cereal and feed for the animals. Every acre was fenced and Dad would rent lots of different sizes along the St. Lawrence River. We had two horses: Piton and La Belle. She (the latter) would pull the sleigh to go to church on Sundays."

Gabe's Uncle Michel, Louis' brother, in October 2014

Working on the DEW Line

After initially working with his father, Louis soon sought work away from home. In 1955 and 1956 Louis worked on the construction of the Distant Early Warning (DEW) Line—a series of Arctic radar stations commissioned by the US Government during the Cold War. His brother Michel recalls stories Louis told of his experiences in the Arctic.

"The US Air Force Globemaster cargo planes would land at Mont-Joli to pick up special cargo and the work crews. The work schedules up there were gruelling, the isolation factor mind-numbing. Men would work for three months in Frobisher Bay (today called Iqaluit) and the area, fly around in helicopters or travel in Bombardier tracked vehicles, and then return home, south, for a two-week rest."

According to Angélina, doing air-drops on the DEW Line was one of the most exciting jobs Louis discussed with her. "He wasn't afraid of anything," Angélina adds.

Head west, young man!

After his last trip to the Arctic, Louis bought a 1957 Dodge Regent taxi and picked up fares in and around Ste. Flavie and Mont-Joli, for more than a year. However, the taxi work soon bored him and he felt the urge to spread his wings.

Unable to make a living on the family farm, and with no aspirations toward the life of a *cultivateur* (farmer) he told his mother that he was leaving for points west. He dreamed of striking it rich in the oil fields of Alberta.

In the summer of 1958, Louis drove off on his 4,500-kilometre journey with one army-style duffel bag, the clothes on his back, and a few dollars. His route took him through Montreal and Toronto and on through Sault Ste. Marie, Fort William, Dryden, and Kenora. By the time he reached the Manitoba border, the difficult road conditions had taken a toll on his blue 1954 Mercury Monarch Lucerne convertible, which he had become so fond of. The mechanical difficulties forced him to stop in St. Boniface. Despite this minor setback, Louis was somewhat heartened by the assurance that he would find "*des Canadiens français*" (French Canadians) there.

Passers-by introduced themselves to Louis and asked about his intended destination. Learning that he had no plans to continue further until he could find employment and a salary to help him cover the costs of a mechanic, they quickly pointed him to the Tourist Hotel. "You would do well to look for Monsieur Bourbonnière," they told him. "You'll find him there, for sure. I bet he'll give you a job."

"*Merci beaucoup*! Thank you very much!" said Louis, grateful for the advice. And if nothing else, he could always find a cold beer at the Tourist, or three...

Louis made his way down Provencher Boulevard to the Tourist, an establishment where instant friendships were developed, and a place to find a helping hand. Many of the men from the neighbourhood would meet there for drinks, cards, shuffleboard, or simply to solve the world's problems, one at a time.

With only forty dollars to his name, Louis landed his first Winnipeg job that same day. He was told to report to the shop of Mr. Bourbonnière's North Star Sandblasting and Painting in the morning. His new employer invited Louis to stay a while with him and his wife, who eventually found him room and board with a family friend.

Louis and Angélina

One day in 1958, Louis was invited by a couple of friends—Mr. Lajoie and Henriette Palud—to join them at Angélina's house to watch television, a hobby that had recently gained in popularity.

Upon entering the house, Henriette introduced her friend.

"Louis, this is Angélina."

Angélina explains today that their new friendship was fun, but not really what would be called "madly in love."

"We never went out alone; he would visit and we would meet *au salon* (in the living room), and we would listen to my parent's gramophone, which was quite a luxury for them at the time. We listened to country music and other hit singers: Paul Anka, Marty Robbins, Johnny Cash, The Everly Brothers, and Ricky Nelson... Watching movies was also a favourite. The most memorable one being *Springtime in the Rockies*, a 1942 Twentieth Century Fox Technicolor movie starring Bettie Grable and John Payne."

Louis proposed to Angélina, and they were married in March 1959.

Louis carried Angélina over the threshold of their first residence, the upstairs apartment of a two-storey house on Aulneau Street, a quaint street in the heart of St. Boniface.

The couple would later move to the first floor of a house on Provencher, not far from the fire hall.

Setting roots in Winnipeg

Louis, "*le petit joker québécois*," had built a solid reputation during his first year in St. Boniface. The employees and customers of Northstar Sandblasting admired him for his work ethic and his energy. According to his brother Michel: "Louis was a hard worker, an honest man, and he was very well respected by everyone who knew him, be they friend, customer, or boss. Nobody could work faster than he could, and do the work with such attention to detail."

Industrial sandblasting and painting, which remained Louis's profession throughout his working life, was (still is) hard and dirty work. Claudette, Louis' daughter, explains that sandblasting, as its name implies, uses high pressure to propel silica sand against the work surface—whether stucco, lamp posts, or other items—to remove contaminant such as rust or scale.

"That hose puts out a lot of pressure and can literally kill a distracted or inexperienced operator who were to drop the hose. Accidents happen," she says. "Operators have lost limbs, severed by the pressure of the jet of sand."

Claudette remembers working with her dad and having to "hand-bomb" (lifting and transporting everything by hand) semi-truckloads of fifty-pound bags of silica sand. Her eyes light up, her voice moves up in pitch, and her rate of delivery increases at the opportunity to discuss a trade that everyone in the Langlois family—except Gabe, perhaps—knew intimately. Gerry, Rob and Rick still work in sandblasting and painting.

On a few occasions Louis dispatched to the Maritimes for special projects. He took the opportunity to bring Angélina on one such assignment, leaving her and the two boys, Mike and Rick, in Ste. Flavie for a visit, while he continued on to Nova Scotia.

To supplement the family income, Angélina worked for Jay-Dee Products Ltd., a cresting and embroidery company, where she cut out the crests, for a Mr. Schacter. Thankfully she could work from home after having kids. Boxes of crests would be delivered to her house and she would busy herself with scissors, cutting embroidered crests and iron-on crests from their master sheets of material.

The missing car episode

"*Allô*, Police!" Louis began upon hearing the constable pick up on the other end of the line. "I would like to report a missing car."

The officer noted the pertinent information and assured Louis that they would call him, should they find anything.

"*Merci beaucoup*," was all Louis could think of saying. "Thanks!"

Scratching his head, trying to clear the cobwebs still lingering from the night before, try as he may, Louis could not remember where he last saw his car.

"Angèle," he called after his wife, "I'm going to go for a walk and pick up the paper."

A few minutes later, walking by the neighbourhood police station, he spotted a familiar looking vehicle in the parking lot: his missing vehicle. The sight of uniformed policemen and police cruisers cleared the fog instantly. Louis remembered leaving it there the night before, convinced the vehicle would be safe by the station, and confident he would be able to find it in the morning. He walked in and apologized profusely to the constable on duty—everyone had a good laugh!

Uncle Michel, Angélina, and Louis sharing a laugh

"That's just Louis," Angélina chuckled. Louis' personality and his sense of humour certainly endeared him to his clients and his friends.

Louis was drawn by the enjoyment of spending time with friends, telling jokes, laughing. He loved to play shuffleboard, cards, bingo, and to have a few beers. He was well liked by everyone and the appreciation he felt drew him out even more. On several occasions, after a few beers "*au rendez-vous des bons amis*" (the rendezvous of good friends) at the Tourist, at the urging of his friends, Louis would do what he enjoyed most, make people laugh.

"My Dad was funny," says Rob. "He also had a bit of a temper, but most of all he loved to laugh, even at work," Rob continues. "He was funny as hell. If you were looking for my Dad, he was always in the centre of laughter. There were always people laughing around my Dad."

Louis loved being the centre of attention and receiving compliments, and those around him visibly enjoyed his sense of humour, his joie-de-vivre, and his company. He spent most weekday evenings socializing.

"I've seen grown men laughing to tears while Louis told a joke, for the third time," recalls Angélina. "He was always the life of the party."

Building the family business

In 1963, Louis invited his eighteen-year-old brother Michel to come west to find work. He arrived at Winnipeg's Union Station at 8:45 a.m. on August 16, and was hired by the time the Union Station clock struck noon. Michel would soon learn the intricacies of sandblasting and painting, alongside his brother.

Louis eventually left Northstar to work for Fort Rouge Decorating and Sandblasting, but he and Mr. Bourbonnière remained friends. In 1973, Louis became increasingly unhappy with his work and his relationship with his new employer soured. One afternoon, Louis and his oldest son, Mike, were picking up Angélina from her work. Louis parked the car.

Mike watched his father enter the Jay-Dee Products building at 43 Westbrook and stepped out of the car to enjoy the warm afternoon sunshine. The paint on the facade of the adjacent building had been weathered by Winnipeg's cruel northerly gales of its long, cold winters, and by the harsh sunlight of its long, hot summer days. A gentleman, curious to know what this thirteen-year-old boy might want, approached him.

"This place could sure use a paint job," blurted out Mike, smiling and brimming with confidence.

The topic surprised the man. Now quite interested in this teenager's opinion, he replied, "You're quite right, young man! You know something about this business of painting?"

"I know just the guy who could fix your place. Best there is. Guaranteed!"

He turned and ran to the car. "I'll be right back!" he called to the man.

Angélina was already seated in the passenger seat when Mike reached his father's window, out of breath. "Dad, you gotta come with me. There's a man over there who wants to talk to you. Come!"

Intrigued, Louis followed his son. The ensuing conversation would change the course of the next ten years.

"Monsieur Langlois, you think you can make this place look like new again?"

Louis took a quick look at the building and replied, "For sure, it wouldn't take much."

"Well, I'm interested," the man said. "When can you get me your quote?"

Mike jumped in, much to Louis's dismay. "We can get you a quote tomorrow, sir."

"Tomorrow!" Louis thought. But not wanting to disappoint his son, he agreed with him. "Yes, I should be able to figure out a price by tomorrow. Would that be fine?"

"I'll be waiting for it, right here" said the man, pointing at the building, as he walked away.

Louis and Mike prepared the quotation that evening and Louis returned at the end of the following day. The man looked at the sheet that described the work, estimated the time required, and stated the price: $800. Louis secured his first client.

Louis Langlois never looked back.

Raising a family

The first three Langlois siblings, Mike, Rick and Gabe were born when the family lived on Burns Way (what is now called Lagimodiere Boulevard). Needing more space and considering the need to be closer to the schools as the kids got older, Louis and Angélina then decided to rent a two-story house in Winnipeg's Norwood Flats, on Chandos Avenue. Eventually, at the end of the summer of 1969, they would move to Hull Avenue where Gabe still lives today with his mom, Claudette, Gerry and Ryan.

The children spoke French at home all the time. In fact, they didn't speak English until moving to Hull Avenue. They attended Précieux-Sang, St. Eugène, Christ the King and Holy Cross schools. Slowly the kids learned to speak English, which eventually became their usual language.

Angélina explains, nostalgia in her voice, "Much to Louis' chagrin, and mine, the kids lost their French slowly." The eternal optimist adds, "but never totally."

With six children joining the family in quick succession, family life could be chaotic at times. As Gerry remembers, "I think the toughest thing for my Mom was all the fighting, amongst ourselves, the siblings. She could not tolerate that. When Mom got mad, you knew it. Mom used the broom until it cracked." As Gerry speaks, he imitates the sound of the cracking broom.

"'Get in the house!' Mom would say, not really screaming," says Gerry. "If that did not achieve the desired effect, then she would come out swinging with the Sher-Wood PMP5023 hockey stick!"

Louis would come home for supper shortly after five o'clock, after meeting with his friends for a beer at the Tourist on the way. Louis would first take a bath, eat his dinner (which was always ready) with or without the kids, but always with Angélina.

"Louis, how come you don't stay home tonight? I'm sure the kids would like to see you, spend some time with you."

"You know, Angèle, if you hadn't brought it up, I bet I would have forgotten about going out," he said with a chuckle. "I'll see you later, *Salut!*" Out he went, to meet with his friends

Another time, Angélina reminded Louis of a promise. "Louis, why don't you stay home? You said that you would stay home more, once the kids could all walk."

"You know I have to go, Angèle."

In the Langlois household, weekends were a time for family and for recuperating from a hard week at work. Saturday was the day for

GRANDPARENTS ON THE SCENE

Angélina's parents, Daniel and Marie-Louise, were fond of their many grandchildren—and they enjoyed looking after Gabe when Angélina needed a break. Grand-maman Dumas loved to spoil Gabe, while Daniel could sit on the floor for hours, playing card games that would test Gabe's amazing memory. Daniel did not mind losing to his grandson.

Gabe's maternal grandparents, Marie-Louise and Daniel Dumas

Angélina remembers her father's last few months, at Taché Centre where, during family visits, Gabe showed a particular passion for the common room's piano. "The residents enjoyed Gabe's music, for a while, but eventually one of the staff came and closed the lid."

On Louis's side of the family, the visits of the Langlois grandparents, were cause for celebration. They first met Gabe in 1966 when they visited Winnipeg for the wedding of Michel, their youngest child, and Lorraine Beaumont. A whirlwind of activity, their visits included so many things to do in so little time. Dinners prepared by Angélina offered perfect opportunities to spend time with their grandchildren and to meet Angélina's parents

The Langlois grandparents visited Winnipeg twice more, when their son Michel took ill, and again in 1979. Gabe only recalls meeting his paternal grandparents for the first time in 1979. "They brought a jar full of pennies, lots of pennies. Dad checked them to see if any were collectors' items, but he didn't find any," laughs Gabe.

Gabe's paternal grandparents, Zénon and Antonine Langlois

"The Langlois family, they had a reputation in the St. Vital community as a hard working family. Monsieur Langlois was such a friendly person and hard working. I remember seeing his big white St. Vital Sandblasting truck drive by. He was so funny, and spoke with a really thick French accent."
—Jill Mathez, Gabe's high school classmate

groceries, housework, household chores, and repairs; Louis could get these done very quickly with the kids' help. Sometimes, when Louis had to work on Saturday, Angélina would do the groceries with her six kids in tow, often on foot. Sunday was the day for church and family outings. Louis loved to take the kids for drives up to the Fair in Lockport for its rides and games, or to Birds Hill for its beach and park, or simply to buy the kids a treat, a pop, or an ice cream cone.

According to Uncle Michel, "For Louis, the well-being of his family always came first. *Il aurait pu donner sa chemise.* He would have given them the shirt off his back."

Louis' passing

"I didn't remember Louis ever being tired," says Angélina, recalling the year 1982. "But he started sleeping in, and I would have to wake him up. I never had to do that before." Louis never missed work. But now he had lost his interest, his energy and his passion for friends and for going out.

"I knew something was wrong," Angélina says, "but Louis thought he would get over it. And he didn't like doctors." When his condition failed to improve and he developed a sore stomach as well, Angélina finally convinced him to see the doctor with her.

After a battery of tests, the doctor explained, "I think your condition is psychosomatic. It's in your head. Your blood is low but not quite anaemic." He gave Louis no prescription, and for his sore stomach he recommended Phillips milk of magnesia.

LIFE ON HULL AVENUE

Gabe's teenaged nephew, Ryan, provides a unique perspective of life on Hull Avenue, where he lives with Angélina (whom he affectionately calls Mémère, or Grandma), Gabe, Gerry, and his mother Claudette.

"Sometimes it can be pretty hectic," says Ryan, who referees hockey, plays football, and has his own busy schedule. "Around the holidays we spend a lot of time cleaning up to get the house to Mémère's standard, which means spotless.

"My uncle Gabe always remembers to wake me up every morning at 7:00 am, sharp! He never misses," says Ryan, who probably wishes his uncle would forget, at least once, and let him sleep in. "He keeps coming back until I get up."

"We sit across from each other at breakfast, always. Sometimes Mémère makes something special, like pancakes and bacon. Other times Gabe has cereal and toast, or he'll often make himself bacon and eggs. He's a good cook—self-sufficient when it comes to food."

Ryan speaks about Gabe's demeanor in the rhythms of a week. "His mood follows the teams' performance. He gets sad, broody. But the next day usually he's ok," he says. "But he doesn't get mad, really. He does get frustrated. He does chores around the house; often he sweeps the floor. He gets frustrated with sweeping, maybe from all the coaching he gets from my Mom or Mémère." Ryan chuckles. "He definitely likes to do his own thing."

Ryan points out that Gabe is particularly close to Claudette, helped by the fact that they still live under the same roof. "My Mom, she's definitely his 'big' sister in many ways (although she is smaller and younger than Gabe). She helps out a lot. She's very busy but she's always there for Gabe."

A few weeks later, in July, Louis noticed a long red and bluish bruise the length of his arm. He did not feel pain. But he remembered that afternoon at the shop, inadvertently hitting his arm against some cupboards he was painting. The bruise seemed to be a perfect match to the area of the cupboard Louis had hit, almost as if it had been imprinted on his skin, like when branding a calf.

"Look Angèle, that doesn't look real nice," he said, concerned.

Nobody slept very well that night. Louis' night was filled with dreams, tossing and turning. Angélina lay awake for most of it, praying, asking God with all her heart to heal her husband.

When he finally got out of bed and made his way to the washroom, Louis felt pain in his arm. He awkwardly turned on the bathroom light and took a look. The entire arm had swelled to twice its normal size, and a red blotch raced from Louis' wrist to his armpit. He could hardly bend the elbow or the wrist. Finally, he walked back to the bedroom where Angélina had fallen asleep and shook her gently.

"Angèle, it's my arm. I think we should to go to the hospital."

Something had to be really wrong for Louis to want to go to the hospital. They arrived at Emergency at the Saint Boniface Hospital by 7:30a.m..

Louis was lying on a stretcher, with needles and IVs stuck in him, when the doctor met the couple at the end of the exhausting day.

"How do you feel Monsieur Langlois?"

"Lousy, but thanks for asking," Louis said. "I want to go home."

"Monsieur Langlois, I'm afraid that won't be possible. The tests show without a doubt that you suffer from leukaemia, a type of cancer that usually begins in your bone marrow."

Louis became extremely agitated at this revelation, pulling at the tubes and needles, and removing bandages. Angélina could not get him to calm down. The nursing staff had rushed in and were doing their best to quiet Louis but nothing worked.

"I cannot stay in here, Angèle. I need to go home. Angèle, I want you to stay with me. You can be my nurse. I don't want these people to touch me; you know I don't like these people."

"But Louis, how can I do this? They are the professionals. They know what to do. They will take good care of you."

But Louis would have none of it; he disliked medical professionals. Again, he became almost hysterical. He refused to be touched by a number of the nursing staff and demanded that Angélina stay at the hospital to administer care to him. It was arranged that Angélina would spend her time at the hospital, even sleep there, and look after Louis: his very own nurse, just the way he wanted it.

Claudette regrets that her dad had to suffer so much during his days at the hospital. Still, his illness did not dampen Louis' sense of humour.

"He had all the nurses laughing," says Claudette.

Angélina would work alongside the hospital's nursing staff over the next six months, managing Louis' morning routine. She would get her meals at the cafeteria when she could find time, but mostly she would eat at home. "Cafeteria food is very expensive, you know," Angélina recalls.

She would go home in the afternoon, shower, change, prepare some food for Gabe and Claudette, coordinate the household chores, check on Gabe, and return to the hospital.

"Gabe knew Dad was sick, but he didn't seem to understand that Dad wasn't coming back. Gabe did not show emotion," according to Rob.

During Louis's stay in hospital, the doctors looked for a match for a bone marrow transplant. After some tests performed in Quebec City, they had determined that Louis' brother, Zénon, was a match, and Zénon immediately made arrangements to come to Winnipeg.

Unfortunately, the procedure would never take place. On Tuesday, January 18, 1983, before Zénon was able to come, Louis J. Langlois, with his family at his side, attempted one more smile and closed his eyes for the last time. He was forty-eight.

"I cried when Dad died," says Gabe. "I was very sad. I felt empty inside when Mom explained that Dad had died."

Claudette adds, "It was very difficult for everyone. We were all shocked. So many people came to his funeral."

Angélina visited the oncology ward once more to retrieve Louis' things and to thank the staff for their care, patience, and dedication. "They had really been very kind to Louis; he had not been an easy patient," she says.

When she had put on her heavy winter coat and hat, the nurses surrounded Angélina. Each of them wanted to hug her and tell her how much they had appreciated her strength, her courage, and her patience. One of them gave Angélina an envelope. Inside was a card signed by all the nurses. "Thank you for your help. You were the best nurse we have ever met."

Taking care of business

Claudette recalls the difficult months that followed her father's passing. "Mike did a lot after Dad died. He wanted life to continue and the family to remain strong. He bought presents for everyone the following Christmas and made sure we were together." Louis did not have life insurance, and with a second mortgage on the home, Angélina needed her children's help to take care of the family's financial burden and to keep running the business, for which all the Langlois children except Gabe now worked.

"We took half-pay to pay the bills, to cover the mortgage, and everything else with Dad's company," explains Rob. "Our creditors also gave us some breathing room."

Mike and Rick took charge of the family business, under the same name. In 1987, however, they experienced significant financial troubles that forced them to sell the company's assets to pay their creditors. The business closed, and the two brothers moved on to other jobs.

Angélina, the survivor

The new millennium has not been especially kind to Angélina Langlois.

In 2004, after being diagnosed with an especially aggressive cancer, Angélina put some order in her affairs and decided to visit her son Mike and his family. After a month's rest and her son's care in California, Angélina returned home for chemotherapy treatments that sent the cancer into remission.

Then, in January 2007, Angélina woke up in a coughing fit. She was able to get Gabe's attention and asked him to call his brother, Rob, who she thought might be home. Gabe dialled immediately. "Rob! Rob! Come quick, Mom's sick!"

In a flash Rob arrived and took his mom and Gabe to the hospital where the staff performed a battery of tests. The doctor met her at the end of the long day. Lung cancer.

Angélina did not know what to say, but to her, it seemed that her life just flashed before her eyes. She had been a smoker for a long time. She lived with smokers. Cancer had taken her husband and several of her friends and relatives. But it was difficult to think that it could happen to her. Medication had reduced her cough but not eliminated it. Angélina could feel herself weakened and irritated—hardly normal for a woman who had been patient, calm and understanding all her life.

Claudette, Angélina, Gerry, and Rob in 2012

After a month without news, Angélina called the hospital only to be told that she would have to wait a little longer for her appointment concerning treatment.

When another month passed without a call, Angélina took the bus to Saint Boniface Hospital and made her way to the oncology department.

"I'm not leaving before I see a doctor," she said softly, her voice wheezing.

Angélina recalls the events as if they happened just yesterday.

"I wasn't leaving, they knew that. So the doctor got my file and realized that I had been waiting for more than two months already. I didn't want to die without seeing someone. He referred me to the best at Health Sciences Centre, and three days later I received a call from CancerCare."

"Then I saw Dr. Maksymiuk. After the required tests, blood cultures, X-Rays and CT-Scan, the doctor informed me that they had found a golf-ball-sized tumour in my left lung, and that I would need to undergo a full regimen of chemotherapy."

Every weekday, for almost eight weeks, Rick, Claudette or Angélina's sister Denise would drive her to CancerCare for her treatment.

A year later, during the summer of 2008, Angélina began experiencing painful headaches accompanied by dizziness and blurred vision. She underwent a new battery of tests, only to learn that the tests showed two brain tumours. The doctor, however, had some good news along with the bad: Angélina's history and her health made her the perfect candidate for this new technology called Gamma Knife Surgery (GKS), a powerful, minimally invasive neurosurgical procedure. (Without a scalpel and without the usual risks of open neurosurgery, most patients return home the same day and resume full activities within one or two days.)

In August, Angélina underwent the surgery and returned home the same night.

Health concerns were not over, however. Later that year, Angélina fell and broke her hip. She had to spend four weeks at Seven Oaks Hospital.

And in June 2012, during a routine test, doctors discovered tumours in Angélina's right lung. They were removed via laparoscopy and Angélina subsequently underwent a number of chemotherapy treatments. She has been cancer-free ever since.

"She's a tough lady," says Ryan, her grandson. "She's been through a lot but she always believes she'll come out on top, no matter what." And she has, so far.

"When she got sick, with lung cancer, I think I was old enough to understand that she could be in big trouble. You could tell by Gabe's face that inside, he was hurting. Gabe always asked—he still does today—'Are you ok Mom?'"

"Mémère would say yes, even if she was half dead."

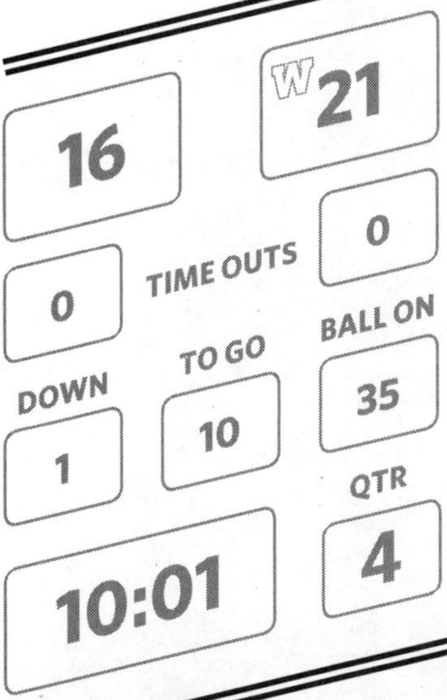

FOURTH QUARTER

NOT JUST AN ORDINARY GUY

BISON
Reebok
DANCING GABE
50
50
50
Reebok

CHAPTER 19

Marathon Gabe

> Don't walk ahead of me, I may not follow. Don't walk behind me, I may not lead. Walk beside me, and just be my friend
>
> —*Camus*

"Running was a big thing for Gabe," says Claudette. "Mom asked Gabe if he wanted to go to the Special Olympics, but Gabe replied curtly, 'No Mom, I'm not like that!' He was only thirteen at the time."

Gabe instead focused his energy on running marathons, starting with attempting the Manitoba Marathon in 1979. However, when came time to register, he decided against it. "I was too out of shape," confesses Gabe, "so I decided to wait one more year."

He trained hard during the winter and spring of 1980. Then on June 15, 1980 (Father's Day), Gabe woke up early, grabbed a light breakfast, checked the weather and got dressed for his first full marathon.

"That morning, Mom and Dad gave me a ride; Claudette was there too. I was nervous at the starting line," says Gabe.

On a course newly designed by Fred Dawson, Gabe stepped to the starting line, along with the other participants. At seven o'clock, the starter's pistol put the mass of runners into motion. Gabe covered the first few miles in good time, feeling energized, but pacing himself. By the time he reached Assiniboine Park, he had slowed considerably but remained determined to continue.

The winner that day, Frank Richardson, completed the race in a time of 2:15:17. As Richardson crossed the finish line at the University of Manitoba, Gabe ran by Polo Park at Mile 13, struggling through the physical and mental demands of such a race. His calves were seizing up, but he soldiered on for another five miles, encouraged by numerous bystanders. Exhausted and in pain, he walked the last few steps to Mile 18 on Lyndale Drive. Exhausted, Gabe had to face the inevitable and stop. He ended his first attempt at a full marathon in the embrace of his mother, who had followed him and encouraged him at every step.

"I'm so proud of you, Gabe," said Angélina.

"Thanks, Mom!" was all Gabe could answer, disappointed.

He gave the full marathon another shot in 1981, cheered on by his mom and dad again. After another valiant effort, the course got the best of him once more as stiffness in his legs became too much. On this attempt, however, Gabe covered twenty-two miles in just over three hours. Determined to prove to himself that he could reach his ambitious goal, he trained hard and registered for the Manitoba Marathon the next year. Gabe tells the story with great pride.

"I finally finished the full marathon! Yeah! In four hours and thirty-nine minutes. There was a big crowd waiting for me to cross the finish line at the University of Manitoba stadium."

But there is also sadness in his voice.

"Dad was sick in the hospital. It was a wet marathon that year." Gabe recalls. Then he adds, "Julie Armstrong, from Windsor Community Centre, ran with me."

The year his father died, 1983, Gabe finished the full marathon once more, on Father's Day. His time, again: four hours and thirty-nine minutes. Consistency has always been important to Gabe.

From 1984 to 2009, Gabe settled for the half-marathon every year except 1997, when an infection sidelined him. All told, he participated in four full Manitoba Marathons and twenty-five Manitoba Half-marathons. Additionally, Gabe participated in the Winnipeg Police Service Half-marathon in 2006, 2007 and 2008. He also ran the Child Find 5-kilometre Run and finished in second place!

Wise Guys' Bob Sokalski, whose house was located along the course near the halfway point of the Manitoba Half-Marathon, tells an amusing story about Gabe and the 2008 Marathon.

"I set up a refreshment station, not necessarily serving your typical 'marathonian' refreshments," he says with a wink. Former Winnipeg Blue Bombers kicker and CFL Hall-of-Famer Bob Cameron—a regular Half-Marathon participant—enjoyed his stop at the Sokalski stand and soon resumed his race. A few miles later, Dancing Gabe passed Cameron, leaving the kicker in his dust. When later questioned by his friends about being distanced by Dancing Gabe, "I guess I shouldn't have had that beer," was all Cameron would say on the matter, according to Bob.

Wrestling

Gabe enjoyed watching All Star Wrestling, earlier in his career. The action captivated him and he did not seem to mind the violence.

"I remember Vern Gagné, the High Flyers, Jim Brunsell and Greg Gagné (Vern's son)," he recalls. "I watched it on TV all the time. I went to a number of live TV tapings. I saw Hulk Hogan around '83 and '86 at the Winnipeg Arena—he was the best!"

Gabe admits that he enjoyed the fighting, the eye gouging, the flying drop kicking, and the rule breaking. "I could do a sleeper hold, a full Nelson and a figure-4 lock," he says, although he confesses never trying these on Claudette.

Finally, Gabe tells of the time when he told André the Giant to leave his opponent alone, who happened to be Gabe's favourite guy. The Giant approached Gabe, calmly bent down to look him straight in the eye, and said: "It's none of your business, kid." Gabe capitulated, and sat down.

Monday, September 21, 1992

On that night, Gabe attended a World Wrestling Federation live TV taping at the old Winnipeg Arena.

"It lasted almost FIVE hours!" says Gabe. He explains that the event's promoter was Bob "Doc" Holiday, who also happened to have been one of Louis Langlois' good friends.

According to local advertisements, the event was billed as "The Ultimate Night Out! WWF Superstars!" The scheduled matches included bouts between Ultimate Warrior and Ric Flair, Macho Man Randy Savage and Razor Ramon, Big Boss Man and Nailz, and Natural Disasters versus Money Inc.

Gabe's passion for running and for wrestling came together at the end of the evening, in an unplanned long-distance run. Brother Mike loves to tell the story. Of course, Gabe is all smiles when he hears the story once more.

On the way out of the arena, Mike says, a group of well-lubricated fans recognized Dancing Gabe and invited him to come along on their school bus. Whether they specified that they would drop him off at home or not, nobody knows for sure. Gabe hesitantly obliged.

After a boisterous ride, the passengers filed out of the bus, at the corner of Logan Avenue and Main Street. Gabe read the illuminated sign on the facade: Occidental Hotel. A few letters, he noticed, were not lit. Gabe was likely not aware of the Occidental's notorious past. As a veteran bouncer, Buzz Baizeley, once told a reporter, "The Occidental was one of the last of the old-time bucket-of-blood bars. I am sure that no patch of real estate in the West beheld more muggings, knifings, bar brawls and murders than that location at Logan and Main."

It seemed to Gabe that the rest of the patrons at the hotel were feeling just as happy as those he rode the bus with. Several of them recognized Dancing Gabe immediately and invited him to party with them.

Gabe could tell he was in a delicate situation; he needed to think and act fast. Everything he had been taught by his mom, all the experience he had gained, was telling him that he was somewhere that he probably should not have been.

Think Gabe! Think!

Gabe went to the washroom without attracting attention, even if relieving himself was the last thing on his mind at the time. He knew that doing so would bring him closer to the front door, and to his escape.

Once out on Main Street, Gabe ran. Running was all he could think of, and he did not stop until he was home. He covered the seven kilometres to his front door in less than forty minutes. Once home, he jumped on the phone and called his brother.

"Mike, Mike!" Gabe shouted in the handset, out of breath, understandably.

"What's up Gabe? You sound out of breath," replied Mike, most concerned.

"I escaped Mike, I got away!"

Almost fifteen years later, Mike relates the story with a smile.

"We couldn't be there for him all the time," he admits.

CHAPTER 20

Gabe at the YMCA

I know that things are missing in my life [because of autism], but I have an exciting career that occupies my every waking hour. Keeping myself busy keeps my mind off what I may be missing. Sometimes parents and professionals worry too much about the social life of an adult with autism. I make social contacts via my work. If a person develops her talents, she will have contacts with people who share her interests.[24]

—*Temple Grandin,* Thinking in Pictures

Judging by the amount of time he spends there, Winnipeg's South-end YMCA could very well be Gabe Langlois' favourite place in town, after the MTS Centre, Investors Group Field, Shaw Park, and home.

Gabe started working out at the Y during his last year at Glenlawn Collegiate. The fitness centre was conveniently located next door to the school. He soon found opportunities to volunteer at the Y and developed quite a reputation for his reliability, trustworthiness, passion, and pleasant demeanour. Over the next thirty years he would earn a solid place on the YMCA team of staff and volunteers, as demonstrated by the numerous awards he received. Today, he talks affectionately of the many friends he has made there.

Sherry Sigurdur, the centre manager at the South-end YMCA, speaks highly of her "Part-time 2" employee (which means he gets up to fifteen hours per week). For as long as she can remember, Gabe has set up equipment for the pre-school youth department, playtime, and childcare. He looks after the bouncer, the small gym, and when

Gabe with Pamela Wright (YMCA Board Chair) and Dave Young (CEO) in 2007. Courtesy of Kent Paterson, YMCA.

required, shovels the snow. After his shift, Sherry says, Gabe works out in the exercise room.

"Honestly, there's nothing to manage with Gabe. He's just a part of it, of the Y. He never misses work without telling us, which usually occurs only when he's got a game or an event to go to."

But it's Gabe's positive attitude that makes him such a treasure. "If only people could be as happy and positive as Gabe, things would be so great," she says. "If only I could bottle it up..." Maybe a new energy drink is in the works.

Floriela at the front counter, recalls a funny Halloween moment. "This big person comes to the front dressed in a full Ironman costume—spandex suit, mask, gloves, and all. Well it was Gabe, of course." She bursts out laughing. "But the best is how he talked with the kids. He asked them how their day was going, high-fived them, and handed out treats."

> "I remember seeing him work and work out. I was impressed by his incredible stamina, especially for running; he's like a machine! Going, going... He is always very upbeat, friendly, and affable. I think Gabe might have even beat our Vice President of Infrastructure (Mike Whalen) once in the half-marathon."
>
> —*Kent Paterson, President and CEO of Winnipeg YMCA-YWCA*

Working!

The grill-covered clock on the wall at the Y's front entrance shows 8:50 when Gabe arrives for work. By the way he moves about, resolve in his step, focus in his eyes, he has obviously done this many times before. He follows a routine that he has perfected over many years.

After unlocking the equipment room, Gabe wheels out the cart where he stored the Bouncer yesterday. The Bouncer is rolled up neatly and tied with climbing ropes that have been knotted to ensure they could be untied easily. Gabe has plugged in the small green fan unit that will bring the inflatable to life. He unties the ropes and unrolls the heavy rubber and nylon structure, no easy task.

Things are in place. Gabe presses the little red rocker switch and the small green fan unit comes to life, first with a soft whir, but then steadies into a much louder whine. The Castle sprouts like a magic plant that has just felt the long-awaited raindrops. Its colourful patterns take

shape as the four spires reach for the ceiling. Gabe then arranges the safety mats at the various exits. He closes the tall curtain that stands as the wall in the middle of the gym. Then he retrieves two small-wheeled horses: a shiny red one and a blue one. He then throws a collection of soft inflated balls, some yellow, some green, for the kids to play with.

The kids run in and immédiately invade the castle, under the watchful eye of Karen Howgate, the director, who attests to the importance of Gabe's work for the eighty kids ranging in age between two and five, who attend the South YMCA-YWCA Childcare daycare.

"They love the Bouncer, and the mini-gym (on Wednesdays)," she explains. "They love Gabe too," admits Karen.

Screams of joy and broad smiles on the faces of the kids and their educators represent the perfect reward for Gabe, knowing that his work brings happiness to all these little ones.

Working out!

Wednesday, December 10, 2014

Dressed for a blizzard, Gabe arrives promptly at 8:30 a.m. and greets everyone at the front desk. He scans in at the staff/volunteer station, and chats with his colleagues. He tells them about his recent Christmas shopping trip to Kildonan Place.

"That seems like a long way to go when you live so close to St. Vital Centre," one comments.

"I go where I feel like going. It's an outing. Sometimes I go to Garden City or Polo Park."

All of this by bus. Tough guy.

"I still have four presents to buy," he says, but will not divulge who gets what. "That's a surprise," he says with his usual boyish grin. He has also been busy "spreading the Christmas Cheer," distributing his always popular and much anticipated Christmas cards.

"I can't believe I'm on Gabe's Christmas card list! It means as much to me as anything else at Christmas, honestly. I love his hand-written notes and personalized message, and the fact that he delivers these live."

—Ace Burpee, Winnipeg media personality (Virgin Radio) and passionate ambassador for the City of Winnipeg

Today, in the gymnasium, Gabe does not set up the Bouncer—it is Wednesday, Arts and Crafts Day—but instead lays out the small play gym for the kids. He makes short work of it and soon proceeds to the change room.

A few minutes later Dancing Gabe walks into the workout room, steps on the treadmill, and stretches, as he does every day, five days a week. Gabe loves routine.

The place appears surprisingly busy to the uninitiated, this early in the morning; it is not even 9:30 a.m. yet. A constant hum fills the air, akin to a factory or maybe a train station. The din comes from treadmills, elliptical machines, bikes, step-climbers, and cross-trainers, but not footsteps; there is no music and very little chatter.

Gabe puts on his headphones and sets the treadmill screen to Shaw TV. Then he enters the parameters in the machine: 45 minutes, 5.0 m.p.h., 0 incline—a rather brisk pace. Gabe presses the Start button and breaks into a comfortable jog.

The machine gets used to Gabe's 250 pounds moving, one step at a time. After fifteen minutes, he increases the pace to 5.5 m.p.h., and takes a drink on the run. Beads of sweat appear on his forehead. The place is getting busier: people come and go, move from machine to machine. But Gabe is focused, a man on a mission.

Gabe's head is starting to bob. Is he tiring? "That's how he dances," says Christine, Health and Fitness Program Coordinator for teens and adults. According to her, it could have something to do with the music he is listening to because now his head is steadier. He has also dropped his speed by a half-mile per hour.

After a cool-down period, Gabe moves to the weight machines, from one station to the next. Each machine becomes an extension of him for his standard three sets of fifteen reps. "One," a loud breath; "Two!" another breath; "Three!" exhale loudly... "Four!" Everyone within a fifty-foot radius can hear, and it brings a smile to newcomers' lips. The regulars have become accustomed to this part of Gabe's routine; some know that Gabe still follows the workout routine instructions from his 1990s *Muscle & Fitness* magazines.

After his three sets, Gabe thoughtfully wipes down each machine, takes a drink, and moves down the line.

His final exercise: running the stairs, twenty times.

Following a final cool-down routine, Gabe takes down the gym on Wednesdays, or the Bouncer on every other day, and goes home.

"Before working at the YMCA I only knew Gabe as Dancing Gabe, just like everyone else. Now I know him as Gabe, my co-worker. Members have come up to me and say: 'Is that Dancing Gabe?' and I say yes and tell them that he works here. They always smile and say: 'That's awesome.' I saw a member the other day point to Gabe and tell his son 'That's Dancing Gabe; you have seen him at Bomber games.' So it's great to know that the younger generations will know who he is as well.

"I feel honoured that I get to work with Gabe and have gotten to know him and who he is, and not just know him as the man who dances at hockey and football games. He is truly a wonderful, caring, and intelligent person and could teach us a thing or two about life."

—Christine Walker, Health and Fitness Program Coordinator at the St. Vital YMCA

Gabe's first bowling team at Dakota Bowling Lanes in 1983/84.
Clockwise from back left: Marc, Tom, Gabe, Cécile, Suzelle.

CHAPTER 21

Bowling

Enthusiasm is the mother of effort, and without it nothing great was ever achieved.

—*Ralph Waldo Emerson*

We know from one of Gabe's evaluation reports while in Portage la Prairie that he liked bowling. Somehow, his involvement in the Knights of Columbus council of Christ the King parish may have helped Gabe take up the sport of bowling. Gabe joined the Knights and enjoyed participating in various community events, volunteering, and volunteering Angélina as well. A number of the members discussed their bowling adventures and Gabe listened attentively, curiously.

In 1983, Gabe had watched bowling on television and decided to give it a try. Why not? "People knew me and were very friendly," Gabe says of his first experience. "Down the middle! They would tell me. I would practice and eventually I got the hang of it."

But where might have Gabe gotten his bowling talents? Angélina admits to liking the sport, herself. "I used to bowl in 1958 and 1959 with les *Filles d'Isabelle* [a Catholic women's organization similar to the Knights of Columbus, which is for men]. I came close to 300 but I was never able to beat that."

Dancing Gabe can be seen bowling at Dakota Bowling Lanes on Tuesday nights, from September to April at 6:45 p.m.. He has been doing this faithfully since the 1983–84 season, and sports quite the record, with an impressive ten 200-point games.

A few years after he started bowling, not satisfied with only knocking down five small pins with a small ball, Gabe decided to join the Monday Night 10-Pin Bowling League at La Verendrye Lanes in St. Boniface. Rain or shine, anytime of the year, Gabe takes the bus to the lanes. He always gets there well before the other bowlers, stretches, and warms up. On game nights, Gabe goes earlier than the scheduled time and pre-bowls to post his score.

After Gabe took up 10-Pin bowling, his uncle Michel gave him a present: his own 10-pin bowling ball and bag.

Spending an evening watching bowling opens a new door into the social life of Winnipeg's Number One Fan. Gabe has made many friends at bowling who appreciate his dedication, his professionalism, and his team spirit. "He's an entertaining bowler, that's for sure! You never really know what's going to happen," says Gil Lavoie, from his post behind the counter. Gil would know, he has been working at La Verendrye for the past nineteen years. "Gabe always arrives early, and he stretches like a pro," says Gil.

Gabe's team, the Hot Shots, includes Al, Bud and his daughter, Natalie, a Special Olympian who won a bronze medal at the 2014 Canadian Championships in Vancouver. She looks like quite the bowler, especially with her bright yellow Tweety Bird bowling ball. When Natalie lines up for a shot, nothing can disturb her focus. Once the ball has been delivered, the Hot Shots know she'll be smiling, regardless of the number of pins knocked down.

Gabe moves to the ball dispenser, picks up his ball and carefully places the appropriate fingers of his left hand—Gabe's a lefty!—in each of the three holes, as he shuffles over to the approach dots. He stares down the lane, holding his ball up, motionless. Then, as if stung by a bee, his body shudders and he steps toward the lane, in something that could best be described as a hop-and-a-skip, at the same time swinging his left arm behind him and extending his right arm to the side, maintaining a precarious balance.

All of this happens very quickly. The ball swings forward, he plants his left foot approximately a meter from the all-important foul line, then the ball arcs forwards and comes down on the lane with a thump a couple of meters down the lane. Gabe has stopped his forward motion, still staring at the ball making its way towards the pins, and now walks backwards, almost moon-walking, until the ball meets the pins and they come tumbling down; the lone 7-pin still standing, much to Gabe's disappointment. He steps to the dispenser, to everyone's encouragement.

Gabe goes through the same routine once more and knocks down the stubborn pin for a spare, to everyone's cheer. High-fives and fist-pumps all around. This happens at least thirty times per evening, every week from September to April. It is always a good shot for the Hot Shots, no matter the number of pins left standing. It is always a good game, no matter the final score.

Bud is quick to comment. "He has a bit of an unorthodox style, quite unique. But he's better than a lot of folks. I love it when he takes his Superman pose, usually after a strike or a really tough spare." Unorthodox to say the least. Gabe's delivery is reminiscent of the famous Fred Flintstone's bowling style, on his tippy-toes, delivering that rock.

One of Gabe's opponents tonight, another lefty, is a tall, lanky, white-haired gentleman with the agility of a ballroom dancer, the poise of a sentinel, and the accuracy of a sniper. His name is Jean Pelletier.

Gabe and Jean Pelletier, in January 2015

"I used to bowl with my right hand before I buggered up my arm," he admits, proudly.

Jean was born on October 25, 1921, and started bowling in 1946 when he returned from the Second World War, where he served with the Winnipeg Rifles in Marseilles, the Netherlands, Italy, and Africa. His bowling partner, Bernice, has also been his life-long partner for sixty years.

"He's a great guy. He's obviously very committed, dedicated," Jean says, as Gabe starts the tenth frame with a strike. "I'm sure Gabe has the best attendance of anyone in the league. He never misses a week."

Another team member overhears the conversation and comes over to offer his perspective." You know, Gabe is a good sport, a great guy. He never does any trouble."

Rose Sylvester, the league's secretary-treasurer tells of Gabe's bowling accomplishments, including his first '200' game back in 2012, and the fact that Gabe was quite excited to receive a crest highlighting the feat.

QUEEN ELIZABETH II
DIAMOND JUBILEE MEDAL

MÉDAILLE DU JUBILÉ DE DIAMANT
DE LA REINE ELIZABETH II

Gabe Langlois

By Command of Her Majesty The Queen, the Diamond Jubilee Medal is presented to you in commemoration of the sixtieth anniversary of Her Majesty's Accession to the Throne and in recognition of your contributions to Canada.

Par ordre de Sa Majesté la Reine, la Médaille du jubilé de diamant vous est présentée en commémoration du soixantième anniversaire de l'accession de Sa Majesté au Trône et en reconnaissance de votre contribution au service du Canada.

Governor General of Canada — *Gouverneur général du Canada*

1952 - 2012

"You know, he's always in a good mood; his score doesn't bother him—he has fun! He says hi to everybody, gets genuinely excited for his shots and everyone else's. There's no doubt he enjoys himself here."

Rose bowls her turn and continues talking of how special Gabe is to her. She recalls the time Gabe brought his Queen's Diamond Jubilee Medal. "He was beaming. Everybody was so happy for him. He's part of the family. It would be very disappointing if he ever left."

48th Wesmen Classic. Wes Lee Coyote, Gabe, and Doran Reid

CHAPTER 22

From Special Guest to the Hall of Fame, Maybe

Success usually comes to those who are too busy to be looking for it.
—Henry David Thoreau

While he is best known for his cheering at the big league games, Gabe has also been a long-time fan of college sports and amateur sports in Winnipeg. He has cheered at University of Manitoba Bisons and University of Winnipeg Wesmen games for more than thirty years, whether at football, hockey, basketball, volleyball, or other sporting events.

Several pages in one of Gabe's scrapbooks document "The Streak," when the Wesmen women's basketball team tied a record that had been set by the UCLA Bruins back in 1974. The Wesmen's streak of 88 consecutive wins came to an end at the hands of the Bisons on December 2, 1994. Gabe cheered that night; he had been there every step of the way.

"He's a treasure for radio. He's always ready, which is great for live broadcast. One time, I was doing a broadcast from U of M and we were on the Bison Jumbotron. I said, "Gabe, I need a word!" on the fly, just like that. With anyone else, you're usually in trouble, but not with Gabe."
—Ace Burpee, Winnipeg media personality (Virgin Radio) and passionate ambassador for the City of Winnipeg

Basketball

Gabe also added professional games to his basketball repertoire during the years the Winnipeg Thunder (1992–1994) and then the Winnipeg Cyclone (1995–2001) were in business. Gabe seldom missed a game. He could be seen at Cyclone games dancing on the sidelines along with the Cyclones cheerleading squad.

In 1997, the Cyclone celebrated Dancing Gabe's thirty-fourth birthday by providing a big birthday cake for everyone at the game to share. Seventeen years later, in December 2014, it was the Wesmen's turn to celebrate their Number One Fan by selecting Dancing Gabe as their Special Guest for the 48th Annual Wesmen Classic.

On the cold and bright morning of the tournament's opening day, Gabe could hardly sit still long enough to eat breakfast. He caught an early bus to the University of Winnipeg. Arriving at the Duckworth

Centre, he found a high school game underway—Oak Park versus John Taylor. He watched the Raiders prevail, with a convincing 79–54 victory over the John Taylor Pipers, to advance to the Metro News High School Boys Classic Final. Gabe wasted no time after the final buzzer to make his way to the floor and congratulate the players.

A few minutes later, Dancing Gabe was honoured during a modest ceremony preceding the tournament's opening game, receiving a souvenir plaque from Doran Reid, the university's Athletic Director, under the watchful eye of Wes Lee Coyote, the Wesmen's mascot. The crowd gave Gabe a warm round of applause, which he accepted with a bow and his trademark thumbs-up sign, before proceeding with the honorary tip-off.

"He definitely adds to the atmosphere. He gets along with everybody and he's not shy. He did a great job at the news conference," said Doran. "You know you're 'big league' when Dancing Gabe comes to your venue."

A place in the Manitoba Sports Hall of Fame

How could Dancing Gabe surpass this latest honour? He has received his share of appreciation, awards and recognition from Winnipeg's professional teams, from his own team at the YMCA, and from local media. From birthday celebrations on the field and at centre ice to being named honorary team captain—not that Gabe seeks all this attention. It seems Kevin Klein might just have the right idea.

Kevin Klein, President and CEO of MyToba.ca, published an online article in May 2014 titled "Dancing Gabe Belongs in Manitoba Sports Hall of Fame."[25] The story, in which Kevin makes the case for inducting Dancing Gabe into the Manitoba Sports Hall of Fame, in the Builder category, was picked up in a Podcast interview on the Tom and Larry Live and on Demand web page.[26]

Tom and Larry strengthened Kevin's case by posting it on their Facebook page, and added clarity—and some laughs—during the interview.

From Kevin's online post:
"I hope you will help me get this done. I have started a petition (you'll find it here: http://www.ipetitions.com/petition/dancin-gabe-into-manitboa-sports-hall-of-fame). Please go here and sign it. Also, below this article is our poll—if you agree say YES and we will keep pushing the powers that be to recognize our friend Dancing Gabe."[27]

Larry begins the Podcast and explains that "11,468 people have seen this post on our [Tom and Larry Facebook] page since we posted it yesterday (May 21, 2014), and shared a number of times." The show's hosts believe that they might have a viral story on their hands.

Tom begins the interview. "Kevin, this is an article you wrote yesterday about Manitoba's beloved Dancing Gabe."

"Yes, my favourite guy."

"Well, he's all our favourite guy, that's for sure. Tell us the story."

"We start to idolize athletes and their success and follow their careers and such [...] There's one guy that is at every sporting event. Doesn't matter if it's football, baseball, hockey, amateur, university. He's always there; he gives 110% every game. Football games at –40 C,

in the rain, and he's doing his thing. He does it because he loves it. [...] Gabe is such a shining example of a sports fan."

"He really is," adds Tom. "There's nobody else like him. He's internationally known, picked up on TV coverage everywhere, whenever he's at one of the games and it's covered beyond our borders. Of course, he's the guy that puts a smile on everybody else's face, no matter what the score of the game."

Kevin agrees emphatically, and continues.

"Exactly. It doesn't matter the score. Has he ever asked for anything? He's just happy to be there, happy to be part of it, happy that people recognize him. He goes out of his way. You see little kids that just love Dancing Gabe and he enjoys that. He goes from section to section in the game; he does more work than Evander Kane!"

Everybody laughs. That is a good one, especially now that Evander wears the Sabres colours.

CHAPTER 23

Dancing With Celebrities

> I was never worried; I had complete faith in him being able to do the routine from start to finish without an error.
>
> —*Stephanie Blandford, Gabe's dance partner on* Dancing With Celebrities

Saturday, May 1, 2010

On this night of the Society for Manitobans with Disabilities' fundraising extravaganza, Gabe has packed his costume and his dancing shoes. He is nervous, very nervous. He checks everything for the fifth time, to make sure nothing essential is left behind. He paces like a big cat in a cage.

"Let's go, Mom, we don't want to be late."

Angélina, Rick, Ryan, and Gabe file into the car and head to the Fairmont Hotel. The annual event, called Dancing With Celebrities, will feature their own Dancing Gabe—as one of the celebrities.

Practice makes perfect

Gabe practiced for this evening for four months, learning dance moves, and preparing to be on stage with some of Winnipeg's best-known celebrities. With Brenda Gorlick as his producer, coach, and choreographer, the odds may have been stacked in Gabe's favour for the evening's competition. Brenda, one of the country's most accomplished actors, singers, dancers, and choreographers, knew how to put on a show and wow her audiences.

"I knew that he was a slightly different-abled person," says Brenda, "that he had a learning disability, that he's a star in Winnipeg terms. But he was largely untrained as a dancer—he moves to his own groove, spirit, and energy. My challenge was to harness that: discover what he liked to do, moves, music."

Brenda chose Gabe's dance partners, Anahid Babaian and Stephanie Blandford, strategically. "I thought it would be optimal to have crew members to work with Gabe. They were students of mine, terrific volunteers, and the fact that they were pretty looking ladies also helped the appeal of Gabe's routine, created movement around him, focused the energy. It all worked out well, created a more involved, embellished dance routine. Gabe looked like a million bucks, and the girls looked really good too in their black skirts, gold sashes, and gold lame booty shorts."

"Brenda called me and asked, and I was 'All In!' I had never met him, I only knew who he was. But my parents were all excited when they found out. They were big Dancing Gabe fans."

—Anahid Babaian, Gabe's dance partner on Dancing With Celebrities

---

"I knew who he was but I never met him. We used to go to Wesmen basketball games—my Mom played for the Wesmen—and Gabe was always there. I was so excited, a little worried; I had no experience with people with disabilities. He made it so easy to be with and to want to spend more time with him. There's just something about him."

—Stephanie Blandford, Gabe's dance partner on Dancing With Celebrities

---

The trio's weekly practices began four months before the event, and their frequency increased as the event drew near. The intense practices demanded a lot from the dancers but everyone fed off Gabe's energy. Anahid is convinced that Gabe practiced a lot more on his own.

Together with Brenda, they developed a gruelling five-minute routine where they could demonstrate their dance skills, energy, endurance, and timing. "He would show up early at every rehearsal, a real treat," Brenda remembers. "He said this event was the most exciting thing in his life. The event would put him in a different light; he was one of the stars of the evening (as he normally is) but this time he was featured as a professional dancer. That was a lot of choreography to learn, and he rose to the occasion."

Show time!

The evening of May 1, 2010 brought much excitement to the Fairmont Hotel ballroom. The competition pitted Dancing Gabe against other celebrities such as Sierra Noble, popular Canadian singer-songwriter, and fiddle player; Justin Swandel, then deputy mayor and councillor; Doug Speirs, *Winnipeg Free Press* columnist and reporter; Indu Brar, manager of the Fairmont Hotel; and singer, songwriter Fred Penner.

Gabe felt a special respect for Fred Penner, whom he had met on a number of occasions. "He's an impressive children entertainer," says Gabe. "I remember a number of his shows at The Forks, Fred would invite me on stage to help him out. I sang The Cat Came Back."

Stephanie describes the hours leading to the performance: "Everybody looked like a million bucks. Gabe was very excited. Shaw TV was there, big celebrities, dressed rehearsal prior and Fred Penner was there, Sierra Noble (I am big fan of hers. I must admit, I was a little star-struck). Gabe was always the centre of attention; everyone wanted to talk to him."

At the appropriate time the lights are dimmed, the crowd hushed. The master of ceremonies takes his place and announces: "Performing the most extensive compilation of classic and contemporary dance moves, over the past sixty years, this is "The Evolution of Dancing Gabe."

Right on cue, clad in an Elvis-like white suit, complete with bell-bottom pants, shiny white belt, gold cuffs, wide lapels and a shirt open down to the middle of his chest, Gabe shuffles to position on the dance floor, next to Stephanie Blandford, one of his two dance partners. They stand beside each other, Gabe in a John Travolta-like pose from the Saturday Night Fever fame, ready for the music to start. The crowd is in for a non-stop burst of energy that would last more than five minutes.

"Oh, he was very nervous," recalls his other dance partner, Anahid Babaian, "but he did great. Gabe is used to the public but this was completely different for him."

Perfect set-up for The King

"The only thing I didn't take control of was costuming, and that was really funny. My eyes must have jumped out of my head when I saw Gabe come out in his costume—I was seeing it for the very first time! Wow! I was hoping for something maybe a little bit more contemporary. My friend André Lewis, the artistic director of the RWB, was one of the judges, and he had a similar reaction when he saw Gabe's costume.

Wouldn't you know it, half way through the show, the darn belt starts coming undone. Gabe danced his way right out of his belt. André and I had moments of panic. "Please don't trip, Gabe, please don't fall!"

—Brenda Gorlick

The dance routine, entitled "The Evolution of Dancing Gabe," was inspired by "Evolution of Dance™," by award-winning speaker and inspirational comedian Judson Laipply. It is a fast-moving, quick-changing medley of more than twenty songs. "Of all the years I've been involved with the Society for Manitobans with Disabilities events, Gabe takes the cake," Brenda says. "He performed the longest, the most involved and the most complex dance routine, period."

Part One begins with twisting to Elvis Presley's "You Ain't Nothing But a Hound Dog" and Chubby Checker's "Twist." Switch to the "Saturday Night Fever" hustle, strut and jive to the Bee Gees' "Staying Alive": the strut, the rollin' vine, spinning grapevine, kick and skate, and the most famous Disco Point Winnipeg has ever seen, the hand roll, the Dorothy Chicken—click your heels together and flap your arms, the four point hitch—you know, pointing your right foot forward, then back, then to the right before hitching your knee to the left and turning your whole body to the left, only to start all over again.

"On Show Night, everybody was so supportive of him. Showcasing a multi-faceted individual with a learning disability, dealing with a dancer who isn't a trained dancer—Gabe is self-taught—fits SMD's mission: everybody is able-bodied, your disabilities have to be looked at as 'abilities.'"

—*Brenda Gorlick*

The couple moves to centre-stage and grooves to "YMCA" by the Village People, pointing right then left, all the time both flashing a radiant smile for the judges and the crowd. But before they could sign the four letters, the music changes to the 1974 hit "Kung Fu Fighting" and Gabe and Stephanie momentarily hold the Karate Kid crane pose before executing a vigorous kick. Then Gabe runs to Stephanie, lifts her in his arms, twirls her around and lets her back down—the move looked pro—as the music changes yet again, and Anahid takes Stephanie's place.

Another vintage hit, "Grease Lightnin'," sees the new couple show their moves for a few seconds before AC/DC's "Shook Me All Night Long," then Stephanie returns and hands Gabe a black fedora. He instantly transforms into Michael Jackson, his favourite dance performer. The two dancers perform a series of cross-steps to "Billie Jean" after which Gabe takes centre stage for "Thriller."

Gabe fires his hat into the crowd and the trio regroups in the centre of the dance floor as Styx's "Mister Roboto" begins. They dance like robots, demonstrating their abilities and synchronization—evidence of the long hours of practice—but beads of sweat now show on Gabe's forehead; he's been at it non-stop for two minutes.

Next come "Walk like an Egyptian," the "Bird Dance," and Billy Idol's "Mony Mony." Part One concludes to Queen's "Under Pressure," with some fancy moves and Gabe's shiny belt dropping to the floor, which could have proved disastrous. Then Stop! Both Anahid and Stephanie lean on Gabe for a moment, catching their breath.

Part Two relates to the next part of Gabe's life, when he started dancing at sporting events. The trio moves into a cheerleading rendition of "Take me out to the Ball Game," just as you would see it at Shaw Park on a warm summer's eve during the seventh inning stretch. No sooner is the song over than Stephanie steps away momentarily, only to return and hand Gabe a Sher-Wood hockey stick to the "Hockey Night in Canada" theme song. Our dancers simulate a hockey play where Gabe shoots and scores! Anahid takes the stick away, the music switches to "We Will Rock You," and the dancing trio leads the crowd into its stomping and clapping routine, Gabe showing his fancy footwork and famous "Air Guitar" dance move. As the Brian May guitar solo ends, the girls move closer to Gabe, place a hand on his shoulders, and all point to the ceiling: a victory!

The crowd erupts into a wild and well-deserved standing ovation for Dancing Gabe and his two dance partners.

By the time the music stopped, the trio had been dancing with abandon for five minutes; all the work, the preparation, the efforts embodied in a five-minute routine that simply flew by. Now, all they had to do was await the judges' decision. [Watching the video is strongly recommended. The five minutes will not disappoint.[28]]

Stephanie sums it up well, "We walked on to the stage; the music started; all of a sudden it was over! Just like that! He was having so much fun. He nailed it!"

Despite fierce competition, Dancing Gabe's performance prevailed.

"I was not surprised he won," says Stephanie. "I know he really, really wanted to win; the Society and the judges knew that. He was floored when they announced the results, so happy, and so were Anahid and I. Not everybody can say they've won Dancing with Celebrities. Sierra Noble was very graceful. You know, Fred Penner was pretty suave too. They both could have won, but it was us and Dancing Gabe!"

Brenda also was not surprised by Gabe's win. "Gabe has a real way to get the crowd going. The judges want to see the dancer having the time of his life, and he was! He's a dancing maniac. Floppy belt and all."

In an email, Stephanie (who moved to Halifax, since, to study in neuroscience) recalls the event and the weeks leading to it:

> I was really eager to be a part of something so important, and be able to use my years of training as a dancer and passion for the art for something more. Who better to share it with than Dancing Gabe, who uses his love of dance to brighten the lives of so many every day?
>
> At the end of this first hour together we said goodbye and he gave me a big hug when we parted, I was so surprised, but we've been great friends ever since. I have been constantly overwhelmed with his kindness. He is the most genuinely nice and lovely person I have ever met. He knows more about what goes on in my life than most people who are related to me.
>
> Gabe was always such a joy to be around during rehearsals. Even when he forgot which step came next, or made a mistake in the choreography he remained positive, and never let his frustration ruin his mood. The three of us really made a great team, I knew Anahid from RWB as well, so together she and I were able to create a very relaxed atmosphere where he wouldn't feel shy around (not that he needed it, he is so personable).
>
> The event itself was incredible. It was so wonderful to see so many local celebrities, and local dancers all working together towards a common goal. It was an experience I will never forget. Knowing Gabe and being a part of the event with him has brightened my life in more ways than I ever imagined.

Canada

CHAPTER 24

Game Day with the Goldeyes

> I am convinced that Gabe never sets out thinking, "I'm going to be the show." It's never about him.
>
> —*Andrew Collier, Goldeyes' General Manager*

Friday, August 29, 2014

Gabe is ready to go, on time as usual, wearing his personalized Goldeyes jersey. He retrieves his water bottle from the fridge and grabs his official Goldeyes headphones and his radio. He kisses his mom and puts on his shades, the ones with the bright orange arms. We slip out the front door.

Another beautiful evening for baseball—not hot, and hardly a cloud in the sky. We walk to the bus stop to catch the #14. As usual, drivers on St. Mary's Road honk their horns and yell "Hey, Dancing Gabe!" But Gabe does not hear them this time; he is absorbed in the pre-game music playing in his headphones.

The St. Vital scenery flies by outside the ad-covered windows of the Winnipeg-made New Flyer bus. From our stop at Union Station, we walk toward Portage and Main. Walking by Earl's patio on Main, a group of patrons waves and shouts to get Gabe's attention but again, he cannot hear them over the music in his headphones. I tap him on the shoulder and point at his screaming fans. He waves; they respond. All is well.

In the players' entrance at Shaw Park, Gabe shakes hands with a number of players and other members of the staff. He is part of the family here, as he is everywhere else in this city. He then proceeds to the stands and sits in the right field seats as the crowd slowly files in. The smells, the sounds and the sights of the ballpark conjure some wonderful memories: the popcorn, the hot dogs, and the mini donuts; the crack of the bats, the ball hitting the back of the gloves, and the vendors' peddling their products; the deep green and brick-red of the field, the Goldeyes players in their super-white uniforms, the bright lights and the scoreboard out in centre field. All of this creates the perfect atmosphere for young and old fans.

Gabe makes short work of his bucket of popcorn while keeping an eye on the players warming up in front of him. Fans walk over to salute Gabe and take pictures, others sit and chat for a while. Smiles are the order of the day.

As the Goldeyes take to the field, Gabe moves to the patio in right field where he is greeted by yet more fans. Goldie and Goldette, the team's mascots, come over to hi-five Dancing Gabe, and strut a few steps as fans take their seats. Soon, it's time to play ball!

From the Winnipeg Goldeyes' inaugural season opener in 1994, Dancing Gabe has had an open invitation from the team's owners and management to attend every Goldeyes event. He still remembers the 14–4 win over the Duluth Dukes. "That was the first time Winnipeg saw professional baseball in twenty-three years," says Gabe.

Today, after the second inning, I meet with Andrew Collier, the Goldeyes' General Manager, to revisit those early days. Andrew has been with the Goldeyes since their first day, back in 1994, in a number of roles. He has been the team's General Manager since 2001. He confirms that Gabe has never had to pay for tickets to a Goldeyes game, "He's part of the experience. For the team's ownership and management, it was just the right thing to do." According to Andrew, Gabe provides a lot of valuable entertainment at the park, something the Goldeyes have always delivered.

"He's a huge sports fan and he loves to get the crowd going... without getting in anybody's way. He is personable, respectful, not overbearing," he says.

Andrew speaks of the way Gabe has been a welcome addition to the team family. "Gabe is always happy to say hi to players and coaches. The new players may wonder what he's about but every player and coach gets to know who Gabe is. He's one of us but we don't have to train Gabe. It wouldn't be the same without Gabe. If he's not here, we miss him (which only happens once or twice per season)."

On this night, Gabe seems to delight in the game's leisurely pace, never taking off his headphones, grooving to the music, listening to the live broadcast, watching the action, and cheering. The seventh inning stretch stirs up the crowd as fan service staff—from the top of the dugouts—lead the crowd in a well-rehearsed choreography designed to get the blood flowing to the beat of Take Me Out To the Ball Game. Gabe joins in and gets the folks in his section involved in the action.

The Goldeyes on that particular evening generate little offence in a pitching duel, being limited to only four hits and no runs by the Gary South Shore RailCats, which made for a quiet evening. The game ends at 9:45 p.m.. Final score: RailCats 3, Goldeyes 0.

But Gabe's mood is impervious to the score. He simply enjoyed his evening at the ballpark and the opportunity to interact with the 5,600–plus fans (2014 average attendance) who came out and cheered on their boys of summer.

Autism no barrier

"Gabe has had a very fulfilling life. He's never shown any limitations and he's provided hope to all of us by what he's accomplished, by overcoming challenges, and just by how he is—a wonderful human being, sweet." He adds, "It's also how he is with kids. He treats them well; he cares and always has time for an autograph, a hi-five, or just a smile. Kids love him; they look for him at events."

—Sam Katz, president and owner of the Goldeyes, and former Winnipeg mayor

---

GABE—A FAN OF WINNIPEG

Sam Katz, President and Owner of the Goldeyes and former Winnipeg mayor, admits to being a big Dancing Gabe fan. "I have the utmost respect for Gabe. He's a Winnipeg treasure. He's a beautiful human being who's enlightened us to what's really important in life. Gabe expresses himself and demonstrates how to slow down, enjoy, and embrace life."

Sam is ready to concede that Gabe is easily the most recognizable individual in Winnipeg, no contest. "If I was standing at a bus stop with Gabe, people driving by would wonder 'Who's the guy with Dancing Gabe?'" he adds, with a hearty laugh. He remembers the groundbreaking ceremony for Shaw Park. "Of all the dignitaries present, I think Dancing Gabe is the one who got the most attention."

Sam is a keen judge of Dancing Gabe, the sports fan. "You will not find a better, more knowledgeable sports fan than Dancing Gabe: he knows the stats, he knows the game, and he knows the players!"

Asked about what Gabe means to a sports franchise, like the Goldeyes, Sam Katz explains, "He's a very valuable asset. When he's not there, people notice. I think it's fair to say that you know you've made it in sports when Dancing Gabe is at your event."

But Gabe is not only a sports fan. He's a fan of Winnipeg. He goes well beyond sports; he attends all major community events. "Winnipeg fans embrace Gabe and appreciate him," Sam continues. "In return, Gabe enhances the events. He's made Winnipeg a better place. He's made them (the sports fans) better individuals."

A dedicated baseball fan

Many wonder what Gabe does when a scheduling conflict arises between the Goldeyes and the Blue Bombers.

"I go to the Bombers," says Gabe. Paul Edmonds confirmed this fact. As the voice of the Goldeyes for twenty years, Paul would make it a point to notice Gabe's absence on the air, asking Gabe where he was. They developed quite the relationship over the years, with a healthy dose of on-air bantering and mutual respect.

"We would salute each other at least once per game, when Gabe would make his way to the aisle below the radio booth, behind home plate," explains Paul. That was just our way of showing how much we cared for, and respected, each other. It is very special to me.

GABE'S DANCING BY THE NUMBERS—BASEBALL

Since he started dancing at Goldeyes games in 1994, Gabe attended a total of 222 home games at the old Canad Inns Stadium (formerly the Winnipeg Stadium). With its lower bowl's 24 sections and stairways (when configured for baseball), Gabe covered approximately 2,500 steps per game, for a total of 550,000 steps. At the end of the 2014 Goldeyes season (including playoffs), Gabe had attended a total of 770 games at Shaw Park (formerly CanWest Global Park). With its lower bowl's 29 sections and stairways, Gabe covered approximately 2,156 steps per game, for a total of 1,660,120 steps.

For those counting, that means well over 2.2 million steps—the equivalent of walking from Winnipeg to Ottawa—just at baseball games! That's a lot of stepping plus a whole lotta shaking goin' on... But who is counting?

Reebok
DANCING GABE
91

CHAPTER 25

Conversations with Gabe

A large part of him is really the happy, excited person that everyone sees—his public face—but he also has a more serious, deeper side. He analyzes and understands what's going on.

—Ryan Langlois, Gabe's nephew

Gabe invites me to join him under the screen tent in his front yard on a beautiful August afternoon in 2014. I bring a list of questions to get us started, but I fully expect the big man to lead the conversation from one topic to another. My other interviews had been more focused on certain topics. This time I would simply follow, mindful not to step on his toes.

The result gives one a sense of how conversations with high functioning adults with an autism spectrum disorder sometimes go: wide ranging, seemingly random, big on factual details, often short on emotion. That is not to say that Gabe does not "feel" his life, the world around him, his family, and his contributions within a larger and more meaningful context. Verbalizing it, or putting it into our "normal"—neuro-typical is the term used in the world of autism to refer to people who are not on the spectrum—frame of reference, in a way that we can all understand, seems irrelevant to him.

In Gabe's case, the conversation has its own charm. His replies to questions often sound like well-rehearsed commercials. But they also reflect with the kind of heart that fans have grown to love. Have a listen:

"Do you have a favourite radio station?" I ask.

"I like many stations but I think my favourite is Bob FM, 99.9. It's a combination of adult hits and variety hits." Gabe switches to AM. "But my favourite radio show is The Big Show on TSN 1290, with Troy Westwood, Matt Leibl and Brandon Rewucki, sometimes Hustler and Lawless." That's not a surprise. For many sports fans, the Big Show gets one's day set with the latest sports news with a Winnipeg flavour.

Switching off radio for a moment, Gabe tells of the time he visited Mike in San Diego with brother Rick, eleven winters ago.

The subject had come up in one of my earlier discussion with Claudette.

"Would you believe it?" she said, "when the boys were out at the San Diego Safari Park, a couple from North Dakota came over and said: 'Hey! Aren't you Dancing Gabe from Winnipeg?'" Dancing Gabe fans are found even south of the border!

We reminisce about movies and songs from Gabe's middle school years. Gabe quickly recalls the hit movie *Saturday Night Fever*, with songs "How Deep Is Your Love" and "Night Fever." Good dance songs, we agree.

"That was a great movie. I remember thinking that John Travolta had all the moves!"

Now we return to the topic of what Gabe listens to on the radio. "In the seventies, I grew up listening to disco music. During my time at Glenlawn Collegiate, people called me Disco Gabe." He also recalls listening to the Winnipeg Jets games on CJOB in 1972 with Ken "Friar" Nicolson. "I remember when the Jets signed Bobby Hull to a one million dollars contract."

"Who were your favourite hockey players back then?"

"Guy Lafleur is my all-time favourite!" he says, "but if you're a Jets fan, you have to be a fan of the Hot Line. That was Bobby Hull, Ulf Nilsson, and Anders Hedberg."

The more time I spent with Gabe, the more I realized how much more I wanted to learn about him. My research on autism made me eager to understand him better, to relate to his way of thinking and his feelings, to hear the music that keeps him dancing, and to share it.

After getting to know Gabe over the summer and fall months, our conversations become more personal. I move to a number of more difficult questions, touchy subjects, mostly related to emotions.

"I was also struck, when we walked together, by her seeming inability to feel some of the simplest emotions. She confessed that she had never been able to 'get' Romeo and Juliet ('I never knew what they were up to'), that she was stumped by complex human emotions of all sorts. 'The mountains are pretty,' she said, 'but they don't give me a special feeling, the feeling you seem to enjoy... You look at the brook, the flowers, I see what great pleasure you get out of it. I'm denied that.'"[29]

—*Oliver Sacks, in his foreword to* Thinking in Pictures, *by Temple Grandin*

Friends

"Gabe, what is a friend?" I ask him, point-blank.

Caught a little off-guard, he takes a moment to collect his thoughts. "A pal, a buddy."

"Do you have many friends?"

He nods emphatically.

"Why do people have friends?"

"To talk. To chat."

"Who are the people you consider your friends, Gabe?"

"Bob Sadler [Gabe's special education teacher at Glenlawn] is a long-time friend," he begins, then offers a name I recognize from our conversations about elementary school: "Kieran Johnston was a friend. But I haven't seen him since our days at Christ the King."

A pause, and then comes a long list. "Beau, from 99.9 BOB FM. I grew up listening to him when I was fifteen. Paul Edmonds, Perry

Miller, Jeremy John from City TV, and Dave Wheeler, popular co-host of the Wheeler in the Morning show on CITI FM."

"Gabe, the people you give Christmas cards to, are they all your friends?" I have to ask.

"Yeah!" answers Gabe without hesitation.

"Now you're talking!" But when I ask him for the list, Gabe shakes his head.

"You don't have a list!" I muse, a little surprised. "How do you make sure you don't forget anyone?"

He smiles, touches his temple with his index finger, indicating that the list is all in his head.

"I just know. I don't forget anyone" he says, confident.

I believe him. But just for fun, I ask Gabe to recite the names on his list. The final count: fifty-seven! And Gabe receives his share of Christmas cards as well. There is a lot of love out there for Gabe.

Love

"Gabe, what does love mean to you?" I ask, again putting Gabe on the spot (How many people would ever ask him this?).

He hazards a guess. "A relationship, with your girl, partner."

"Have you ever been in love, Gabe?" I might be prying a little too much here. But Gabe provides a stellar answer.

"I've tried but it's tough." He pauses a few seconds to collect his thoughts, then: "I'm in love with sports, [yes! I say to myself] and "I love my Mom. I take care of her, and she loves me."

Angélina has been listening quietly to what probably feels like an inquisition. She derives much satisfaction and pleasure watching her son field the questions like a seasoned professional. This last answer brings a smile to her face. She nods, approvingly.

"That's very good, Gabe. You know that I love you."

Asked if he ever had a girlfriend or asked a girl out on a date, Gabe answers, a little bashful. "I tried, but I seem to only have bad luck," Gabe admits. But he doesn't volunteer names. I don't pry.

Sadness

"Gabe, tell me about sadness." I ask, a little unsure of the emotions the question may conjure.

Gabe looks at the table and plays with his coffee cup. Then he looks away as he answers. "Losing my Dad a long time ago, eleven days before my twentieth birthday. He died of leukaemia on January 18, 1983. That was very sad.

"Did you cry?"

Gabe hesitates. "I don't remember. I probably did," he adds, a little embarrassed. Angélina looks at me, nodding her head from side to side, indicating that, in fact, Gabe did not cry. This may seem a little shocking to some, but should not be surprising, given Gabe's autism.

Without warning, he continues. "The Great Arena Debate and the NHL salary escalation were really sad for me. The Winnipeg Jets leaving for Phoenix—on 4.28.96[30]—were the saddest for sure. I cried in the dying seconds of the third period. Melancholy."

Claudette's son Ryan would confirm this in a later conversation. "Gabe was heartbroken, he cried so much," he says. "Mémère said that's the most he's ever cried."

"I also cried when the teams missed the playoffs," Gabe adds. "Disappointed." I am ready to move to a happier subject, but Gabe is not quite finished.

"Dad, that was a different sadness," he specifies. "I didn't want to talk about it. It's difficult to know how to relate, how to deal with it. It hurts, I turn it down."

I admire Gabe's composure. He has said enough, and I have nothing to add on the topic.

Faith

"Gabe, what is faith?" I anticipate no beating around the bush on this one. Gabe was raised in the Catholic faith, and goes to church regularly.

"Believe in God, of course," he says, as if I should know this.

"Why do you believe in God?"

"Why?" he asks, incredulously, as if he can't believe I am really asking this. "Because it's good. Sometimes you need to make sacrifices. The Big Guy looks out for you, ensures you are prosperous."

I ask about prayer, knowing that Angélina prayed often and has likely taught her son to do the same.

"Praying? I like to pray," Gabe admits, unabashed. "Our Father. I talk to Jesus when I pray. I also like to pray in songs, like Morning Has Broken and He'll Raise You Up. These are beautiful songs. Soothing."

Potpourri

On another occasion, Gabe and I cover a number of other topics, none of them sports-related. This time Gabe leads out, but the conversation is just as much a potpourri as ever: "The new mayor, Brian Bowman: I like his infectious smile," begins Gabe.

"What does the mayor do?" I ask.

"Speaking, talks, debates with councillors at City Hall. He leads, represents our city, does the budget, and looks after things. He has to be a team player—everybody needs to work as a team."

"Pretty good," I say.

"I couldn't be the mayor," confesses Gabe. "It's no easy task."

Since we are on the topic of politics in 2014, I decide to quiz Gabe about the turmoil within the ranks of the governing NDP Party.

"What happened to Premier Selinger recently?"

"Oh," begins Gabe with a concerned look. "Big time trouble! It's because he raised the Provincial Sales Tax last year." A few seconds pass. I wait in silence for Gabe to continue.

"It's the Rebel Five," Gabe adds. Without missing a beat, he names the five ministers who resigned their post, then gives his final assessment on the topic. "They don't like the Premier."

"Can we talk about the police, Gabe? What do they do?"

"They're good. They get to you when you're in trouble. Good people." Gabe recalls the many times when the local constabulary responded to his distraught mother's calls, and brought him home safely.

"But if you do something bad," Gabe continues, "they'll arrest you." He points an index finger at my chest while his thumb points at the ceiling. "Busted! You're caught!" He laughs, like a big kid. "The police have radios, CBs, but you reach them by calling 911. They have guns, handcuffs, and tasers. There are policemen and policewomen; they are friendly. They make money, but not like hockey players." Priceless, I think.

He goes on. "I met the Chief, Devon Clunis, and Sergeant Gary Mathez, he's Jill's brother." (Jill Mathez was in Gabe's graduating class at Glenlawn Collegiate).

Gabe interrupts himself. "Let's talk about popcorn."

Our popcorn discussion begins with the salty and buttery treat that Gabe enjoys so much—but soon leads to money. When I ask him the price of popcorn at the different venues in Winnipeg, he has the figures at his fingertips and easily rattles them off.

We tackle cancer, a topic that Gabe knows personally, given the fact his mom has fought and survived cancer four times.

"There's lung cancer, skin cancer, pancreatic cancer, brain cancer... There are many more. It's really sad."

"What causes cancer?"

"Smoking. Too much sun tanning. Let's move on," he says, eager to end this discussion.

I try to lure Gabe into predicting whether a particular team will win an upcoming game and will make the playoffs. He just will not take the bait. The man epitomizes the idea of "living in the moment."

"We'll see," is his usual answer to questions like this. When asked which team is the strongest or favourite to win, he provides each team's record, and says, "It should be a good game."

After a tough loss for the locals, I try to draw him in and comment about a bad play or a weak goal, but Gabe resists the temptation to criticize someone's performance. He simply sticks to the facts: how many shots the goalie stopped, how many completions the quarterback made, or how many goals a player scored. Gabe can always find the crocus in the snow, the diamond in the rough. No matter how awful someone's performance was, Dancing Gabe's glass is always more than half-full. His favourite assessment: "He tried hard."

Finally, I decide to ask Gabe how he developed the ability to remember names. "Do you use any special technique?"

"No," he assures me. "I think it was John Batzal who taught me. He was the president of Windsor Community Centre. He's the one who told me to always shake hands, a good, firm handshake, to look people straight in the eye, and to make sure I got their name." Just like that, the secret is out.

I am curious to know if the natural beauty that surrounds us touches Gabe.

"Gabe, tell me about sunsets."

"That's when the sun goes down, and light turns to dark."

"Do you like watching sunsets?" I ask, hoping for a glimmer of emotion, a reflection.

"Once in a while," he admits, coolly.

"They don't do much for you?" I say.

"No, not really," he concludes with a bored sigh. I recognize the signal. We are done.

Time for one last, all-important question.

"Do you ever think about retiring from dancing, Gabe?"

"Nope," is his only reply.

End of story.

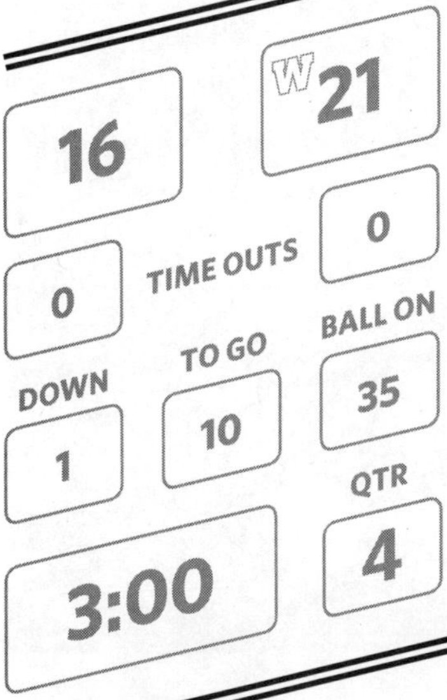

3 MINUTE WARNING

SUMMING IT UP

#1 GABE

EPILOGUE

Dance Like Nobody's Watching

Dancing Gabe has been leading cheers and putting smiles on the faces of almost 24,000,000 fans since 1984—thirty times the population of Winnipeg. At more than 325 football games (well over 2.5 million steps), 1,027 hockey games (5.8 million steps), and 992 baseball games (2.2 million steps), Gabe Langlois has done what he does best: cheer on his teams. Why? Because that is what truly makes him happy and gives meaning to his life.

Every moment of every day is a highlight for Gabe. And maybe, just maybe, that *joie de vivre* is the best gift Dancing Gabe gives those who dare groove, clap, cheer, smile, or live in the moment with him. They know that what he gives, he gets back ten–fold.

But who is counting? For all of his stepping, shaking, and dancing, Gabe's admirers are unanimous, "It's never been about him. It's never been his show."

Jean Vanier was not counting when he founded L'Arche, and discovered that those people whom society typically considers the weakest enable the strong to recognize and welcome their own vulnerability. The new reality discovered by Jean Vanier more than fifty years ago: encounters with people with intellectual disabilities transform us! People who meet Gabe attest to his unbridled passion and enthusiasm, and his natural ability to put a smile on everyone's face, effectively transforming us.

"How the heck did all this happen? How did Dancing Gabe get to be such a personality in Winnipeg?" asks his brother Mike. After all, Gabe never had a coach. What made him do it? Was it sheer determination?

It is important to recognize the role that Winnipeg's professional sports teams and the media played in Gabe's journey. He has received extensive coverage in all media types and has received strong and lasting support from Winnipeg's professional sports teams for well over twenty years. He also received support from many other individuals and organizations.

Gabe's nephew, Ryan, who knows him well, provides another insight into Gabe's motivation. "He's an extraordinary person who's not afraid of being himself; he is very secure. He enjoys going out, seeing and meeting new people. People are surprised when he actually reaches out to them to say, 'Hi, how's it going?'"

And then there is the support of Gabe's family. According to geneticist, Dr. Bruce Blumberg, "Families often do find raising a handicapped child a gift, despite the hardship," he said." It creates new relationships, reveals new capabilities. The trick is to give up the idea of the potential child and accept the actual child."[31]

In Angélina's eyes, Gabe's potential has always been limitless. In her mind, her only role was to make him believe that he could succeed, and succeed he did.

The richness of Dancing Gabe's journey has grown from the love, attention, and caring of so many people in his community, his "village," who accepted Gabe and gave of themselves wholeheartedly, each in their own way. To Gabe's image, the hundreds of people who helped him along the way did so unconditionally—they never asked for anything in return, just like Gabe—and simply because it was just the right thing to do, without seeking gratitude or recognition. They could not know that Gabe's story would become such a resounding success, yet without their support and kindness, the story would have been dramatically different.

In return, Gabe helped create a sense of village in this big city of Winnipeg, possibly well beyond the city's boundaries, simply by the way people engaged with him. Dancing Gabe brings out the best in us without really trying, just by being himself.

The child gives back to the village in innumerable ways.

A mirror for the village, to look at ourselves.

APPENDIX

Gabe's Accomplishments

Milestones and memorable events

This list, taken directly from Gabe's scribbler, contains only minor edits:

1984—Started dancing at Blue Bomber games

1985—First 300-point game, 5-pin bowling

1986—Expo 86 in Vancouver; attended with Claudette

1987—Second 300-point game, 5-pin bowling

1987—My first Grey Cup, in Vancouver

1991—Started dancing, officially, at Winnipeg Jets games

1991—My second Grey Cup, in Winnipeg

1991—5-pin bowling mixed championships and grand aggregate

1992—Started dancing at Winnipeg Thunder games

1993—5-pin bowling mixed Men's high single

1993—Third 300-point game, 5-pin bowling

1994—Started dancing at Winnipeg Goldeyes games

1995—Started dancing at Winnipeg Cyclone games

1995—5-pin bowling mixed championships

1996—Started dancing at Manitoba Moose games

1997—I am named lifetime Honorary Team Captain of the Manitoba Moose

1998—My third Grey Cup, in Winnipeg

1998—Fourth 300-point game, 5-pin bowling
1999—Fifth 300-point game, 5-pin bowling
2002—Sixth 300-point game, 5-pin bowling
2002—My team wins Men's 5-pin bowling championship
2003—Seventh 300-point game, 5-pin bowling
2003—My team wins Men's 5-pin bowling championships
2003—I win Men's 5-pin bowling hi-single handicap
2004—I win Men's grand aggregate
2006—Manitoba Moose release Dancing Gabe Top-5 Moves video
2006—My fourth Grey Cup, in Winnipeg
2007—Eighth 300-point game, 5-pin bowling
2007—I win Men's 5-pin bowling, hi-single handicap
2007—My first ever 10-pin bowling game
2007—I attended my fifth Grey Cup, in Toronto
2007—First ever National Junior Football Championship at Canad Inns Stadium (Saskatoon Hilltops vs St. Leonard Cougars)
2007—Second CIS Playoff run (Bisons)
2008—My team wins 10-pin bowling mixed championship
2008—At my old school (alma mater), Glenlawn Collegiate: The students sang "Happy Birthday Dancing Gabe." 45 years old. Everybody danced to *Soul Jo Boy Tell'Em's Crank (Superman).* It was a Pep Rally (before that there was Spirit Week. That was Spirit Week 2008-2009). Grade 9 was expanded. Packed house at the Coliseum Gym. Grade 9 wore yellow; Grade 10 red; Grade 11 green; Grade 12 blue: United in Colours. Every year since 1999 I attended...
2008—My team wins first 10-pin bowling championship
2009—I star in Winnipeg's Filthy Animals Rap Video (FILTHY ANIMALS in "THE PLOT" feat. DANCING GABE (OFFICIAL VIDEO) https://www.youtube.com/watch?v=bOoaMkvHP_A&list=RDbOoaMkvHP_A#t=266

2009—Ninth 300-Points game, 5-Pin bowling

2010—Won a "Star Performer" Award for Dancing With Celebrities

2011—Winnipeg Goldeyes Tribute to Dancing Gabe at Shaw Park

2011—Face-off Party at The Forks; First NHL game in 15 years at the MTS Centre

2012—First and second 200-point game, 10-Pin bowling

2012—Tenth 200-point game, 5-Pin bowling

2012—Winnipeg Goldeyes win the American Association Championship

2013—Two days before my 50th birthday, the Winnipeg Jets gave me a framed jersey "Dancing Gabe 50." Jimmy Mac was the MC for the event

The milestone birthday! I'll never forget, I was Winni-famous. That was a special day for me. I was on City TV on Breakfast TV. Jeremy John and Courtney Ketchen invited me to celebrate my 50th birthday with them. Jenna Khan was weather specialist. Everybody dancing to Lady Gaga's "Poker Face." I did a "You Can't See Me." After that we went to 92 CITY FM's sister station, 102.3 CLEAR FM. I came to the Joe Show with Joe Aiello. *That's a day I'll never forget!*

2013—Third 200-point, 10-Pin bowling

2013—Blue Bombers play their first game at IGF on 6.27.2013

2013—Met Jonathan Toews and the Stanley Cup at the Jonathan Toews Community Centre

2013—Winnipeg Rifles play their first game at IGF

2013—U of M Bisons play their first game at IGF. It was the first ever Canadian College Football at night (primetime). The best fan experience we ever had. The atmosphere was electric, exhilarating, shocking, exciting, fun! 10,000 fans came to watch the first CIS game at IGF. U of M Bisons beat the U of Alberta Golden Bears 65–41. Unforgettable night!

2013—Winnipeg Blue Bombers win their first ever at IGF, over the Saskatchewan Roughriders, in the Banjo Bowl

2013—Winnipeg Rifles win their first junior football game at IGF

2013—First CIS playoff game held at IGF. U of M beat U of Saskatchewan Huskies 37–36.

2014—Fourth, fifth and sixth 200-point games, 10-pin bowling

2014—I attended my 1,000th hockey game

2015—The Winnipeg Jets make the playoffs, and play the Anaheim Ducks

2015—FIFA Women's World Cup Canada 2015 at IGF

Gabe's medals and awards

1979—Toastmasters Award

1980—Special Award Glenlawn Collegiate—Sports

1983—Most improved bowler (5-pin bowling)—Tuesday Night League at Dakota

1985—Leader of the year (south family YMCA)

1986—5 years of service (volunteer) YMCA

1991—10 years of services (volunteer)

1996—15 years of service (volunteer)

1998—10 years of service (YMCA)

2001—Premier's volunteer awards; presented by Premier Gary Doer—plaque—at Winnipeg Convention Centre with Mom

2003—15 years of service (YMCA)

2004 to 2008—A total of five medals

2006—Honorary Student (Kildonan East Collegiate)

2008—20 years of service (YMCA)

2013—Awarded the Queen's Diamond Jubilee Medal during the Jets final regular season game versus the Habs

2013—25 Years of Service (YMCA)

Volunteering

1990—Western Canada Summer Games

1991—2008, Winnipeg International Children's Festival

1998—Grey Cup volunteer

1999—Pan–Am Games, 99-person relay torchbearer, Opening & Closing ceremonies, Welcome Centre

2002—North American Indigenous Games

2004—2008, Winnipeg Fringe Festival

2007—World Women's Hockey Championships at MTS Centre

Manitoba Marathon and other runs

1980 to 1983—Ran full marathon

1984 to 2007—Ran half marathon

2008—Participated in 29th marathon

1979, 1997. Only two years missed.

2007—Won second place Child find 5-km race

2008—W.P.S. half-marathon

Integral reproduction of the letter written by Gabe's eleven-year-old niece, Chanté Langlois (Mike and Lucy's daughter), as a class assignment.

APPENDIX

My Uncle, My Hero

Dancing Gabe

My uncle is my hero, he has inspired many people and touched the hearts of a million. Your probably wondering to yourself how did he ever do that! Did you know my Uncle Gabe was diagnosed with autism when he was a little boy. He did not speak till he was ten years old. My Uncle Gabe had so much energy that he could not sit still... My grandma often wondered what she could do to help him. One day she decided to take him out to hockey games with his 4 brothers and 1 sister. His oldest brother is actually my dad. My dad was a professional ice hockey referee. He took my Uncle Gabe to hockey games. My Uncle loved the noise and excitement at the games. He had so much energy that he just started to dance, throughout the arena. At first some people did not accept him and now 35 years later my Uncle Gabe has not missed any games... he proudly continues to dance at all the games including professional baseball and football. He is known very well in winnipeg, Manitoba, Canada, as "Dancing Gabe," number 1 fan. He has accomplished great things in his life against all odds he became a celebrity and well known in a city of a million people, as dancing Gabe. He is my hero and inspiration because he taught me in life be all that you can be, and never give up.

Chanté Langlois

ACKNOWLEDGMENTS

So many people deserve my sincere appreciation and gratitude for their help and their encouragements.

Mike Langlois for your vision, your support and your friendship. You planted the seed that would become Dancing Gabe's story and you trusted me.

Michele Taylor and Allan Zimmer for believing that I could write this book and setting the wheels in motion.

Angélina, for welcoming me in your family with open arms and trusting me. You shared so much and retraced the past eighty-five years with me without hesitation, despite the pain certain memories caused. You are truly an inspiration.

Claudette, Ryan, Gerry, Rob, and Rick Langlois for your help and support.

My editor, Byron Rempel-Burkholder, for your expertise, coaching and insistence that I always keep the reader at the forefront of the writing process. You dragged me out of the minute details and ensured I never lost sight of the bigger picture. Your contribution enhanced the story and educated its author.

My friends who volunteered their time to review the manuscripts and provide invaluable advice: Mike Stasiuk, Brock Coutts, Michele Taylor, Larry and Rose Johnston, Chris and Cheryl Enquist.

Mark Chipman for writing the foreword and providing your unique and personal Dancing Gabe perspective.

Sister Florence Vuignier, the Chanoinesses' current community animator, for patiently explaining the intricacies of a life as a Chanoinesse des Cinq Plaies and for making invaluable introductions in Notre-Dame-de-Lourdes.

People who met with me to share their Gabe stories and perspectives, and others who also contributed to this great journey (listed in alphabetical order): Scott Arniel, Anahid Babaian, Bernard Balcaen, Kyle Balharry, Carol Barrott, Denise and Romeo Bélisle, Lucille Benoit, Stephanie Blandford, Edith Boissy and daughters Annie and Monique, Mrs. Annette Bosc and son Gilbert, Mayor Brian Bowman, Sergio Briscese, Ace Burpee, Tim Campbell, Mark Chipman, Kevin Cleveland, Andrew Collier, Dave Crook, Paige Curry, Dionne Deer, Kathy Diehl-Cyr, Charlene Diehl, Denham Dubuc, Paul Edmonds, Tim Flook, Paul Friesen, Gabe's Monday Night Bowling mates at La Verendrye Lanes and the Hot Shots, Gabe's Tuesday Night Bowling mates at Dakota Lanes, Kate Gameiro, Brenda Gorlick, Laura Gretsinger, Tom Halliwell, Karen Howgate, Bob Irving, Mason Juras, Sam Katz, Margaret Kingdon, Kevin Klein, Sister Alice Konefall, Uncle Michel Langlois, John Leggat, Rick Loewen, Glen Lowther and Dale Brownlee, Tara Maslowsky, Jill Mathez, Lynn Miller, Perry Miller, Kelly Moore, Terry Newton, Mike O'Hearn, Roger Pantel, Kent Paterson, Jean Pelletier, Scott Pettigrew, Doran Reid, Julie Reid, Bob Sadler, Sherry Sigurdur, Bob Sokalski, Rose Sylvester, Joan Thomas, Maria Todd, Christine Walker, Cynthia Winram.

Special thanks to Wade Miller and Kim Babij-Gesell of the Winnipeg Blue Bombers; Mark Chipman, Scott Brown, and Kalen Qually of the Winnipeg Jets; Sam Katz, Andrew Collier and Dan Chase of the Winnipeg Goldeyes; Doran Reid and Sheldon Appelle of the University of Winnipeg Wesmen, for arranging access to games.

My sister, Sylvie, for your generosity (*et ton grand coeur*), your patience, and conviction. Your encouragements pushed me to make the change that made this whole adventure possible.

My wife Elaine, my son Chris, and my daughter Michelle. You have been my strongest critics and my fiercest supporters. You keep me grounded, you make me better, and you make sure I never take myself too seriously. You are the best.

Finally, thank you Gabe! You were "All In" from the very beginning. The affection and the respect you have earned from an entire community reflect the joy and happiness you spread, simply by being you. You taught me to be more patient and more tolerant, and reinforced the beauty of living in the moment. You were dealt a tough hand early on; you've turned it into a winning hand. Keep on dancing!

To all of you, from the bottom of my heart, THANK YOU!

END NOTES

1 http://www.samefacts.com/2009/07/everything-else/bleg-quotation-source/

2 *Thinking In Pictures: My Life With Autism*, Temple Grandin, page 72. Quote from Therese Joliffe.

3 Temple Grandin, a famous high functioning person with ASD offers the following on savants: "Many people have been fascinated by the terrific feats of memorization of savants [I do not mean to imply that Gabe is a savant]. [...] Approximately 9 or 10 percent of people with autism have savant skills. Some are like calendar calculators who can tell you the day of the year for any date; others can perfectly play a piece of music they have heard only once. Another type can memorize every street in a city or every book in a library. Savants are usually very impaired in learning other skills, such as socializing." Ibid, Page 184.

4 Gordon Sinclair Jr., in "Dancing Gabe, The Man. Insight into the person behind the moves and ever-present smile," *Winnipeg Free Press*, December 22, 2007.

5 Gordon Sinclair Jr., "Dancing Gabe off to Grey Cup! Take a bow for sending Blue's No. 1 Fan to T.O.", *Winnipeg Free Press*, November 23, 2007.

6 http://www.autismsocietycanada.ca/understanding-asds/what-are-autism-spectrum-disorders

7 Normally, the regular daily routine of a Chanoinesse's life was carried on in complete silence, except when work circumstances required communication. A member of the congregation would read stories from a religious book at dinner time. Sisters would then adjourn to the common room where, for an hour afterward, they were allowed free time for crafts and other activities, and conversation. However, on the day of religious feasts and other joyous occasions, a Grand Benedicamus (large blessing) was decreed, allowing the sisters to celebrate, sing and talk "everywhere," at any time.

8 http://www.larche.ca/en/jean_vanier/biography

9 http://www.faithandlight.org/rubriques/haut/actualites/templeton-prize-release-embargo-11-march-1030gmt.pdf

10 *Winnipeg Free Press*, Monday, April 24, 1972, Page 28.

11 With regard to children, the Wechsler Intelligence Scale for Children (WISC) is the most commonly used test in helping measure a child's mental capacity. Children with autism spectrum disorder, more often than not, require special education to help them improve and develop skills despite their developmental disability.

David Wechsler originally developed WISC in 1949. In 2003, the fourth and latest edition of WISC was published and is presently being used by practitioners to determine intellectual strengths and weaknesses of children ages 6–16. The WISC-IV consists of four different indexes, each with their own subtests. For more information, refer to http://www.special-learning.com/article/full_scale_intelligence_quotient_fsiq

12 *A Happy New year's Day*, Roch Carrier, Tundra Books, Montreal, 1991, Page 1. Copyright Roch Carrier. Quote with permission from Mr. Roch Carrier.

13 The timing differs slightly between Gabe's scribbler and the report in Gabe's file, which states 1:00 p.m. as the time of his admission at Middlecourt.

14 The Metropolitan Readiness Tests (MRT) are designed to assess the development of the cognitive skills necessary for success in beginning reading and math. For more information, see: http://ericae.net/eac/eac0141.htm

15 At the request of Gabe's foster family, to respect their privacy, I did not use their real name in the book. Boissy is a fictitious name, as are Edith, André, Annie, Patrick, and Monique.

16 Premier Ed Schreyer's speech is available at the Archives of Manitoba, Q27492, EC0030, GR6792.

17 Sister Georgette seemed to have an intuitive sense of what Temple Grandin wrote in reflecting on her own autism. "Learning social skills is like learning how to act in a play. Social skills can be taught but social emotional relatedness cannot be taught. Social skills and emotional relatedness are two different things. Often parents ask me, 'Will my child have a true emotional relationship with me?' It is sometimes difficult for parents to accept that the brain of their child is wired differently. A social emotional relationship that is purely emotional may be of little interest to the child. Autism varies widely, and some individuals will be more emotionally related than others." Ibid., Page 164.

18 Archie and His Friends, produced by CKY-TV Winnipeg, was an on-going half-hour series for pre-school children in which ventriloquist Uncle Bob Swartz and puppet Archie Wood entertained children with crafts, animals and birthday telephone calls. Guests of interest to children were introduced frequently. Other puppet characters on the show included Grandpa Wood, Tammy True, Marvin Mouse and Petite.

19 An anonymous comment posted online on the day of Gabe's fiftieth birthday.

20 For further information, see *Exceptional Children in the Schools*, Lloyd H. Dunn (Ed.), New York: Holt, Rinehart and Winston, 1965, Pages 130-131.

21 YouTube posting updated January 29, 2008. https://www.youtube.com/watch?v=O0KaSMLNYVk

22 *The Hockey Sweater*, Roch Carrier, Tundra Books, Toronto, 1970, Page 1. Copyright House of Anansi Press. Reproduced with permission.

23 http://www.familleslanglois.com/ancetres/noel.html

24 Ibid., Page 160.

25 http://mytoba.ca/voices/dancing-gabe-belongs-in-manitoba-sports-hall-of-fame/

26 http://tomandlarry.ca/dancing-gabe-larrys-lady-butt-and-freeze-your-pants/

27 http://mytoba.ca/voices/dancing-gabe-belongs-in-manitoba-sports-hall-of-fame/

28 https://www.youtube.com/watch?v=OeIABVrWtDQ

29 Ibid., Page xvi (Foreword by Dr. Oliver Sacks).

30 When referring to dates, Gabe usually uses only numbers.

31 A gift... Part 2, Chapter 1. http://v1.theglobeandmail.com/v5/content/features/focus/boyinthemoon/part1/chapter4/

SOURCES

Books

Gaborieau, Antoine. *Notre-Dame-de-Lourdes (Manitoba) 1881-1990, un siècle d'histoire*. Notre-Dame-de-Lourdes : Comité des fêtes du centenaire, 1990.

Boisvert, Normand. *Centenaire des Pantel.* Notre-Dame-de-Lourdes : Comité du livre du centenaire, 1991.

Haywood History: 1907 – 2007, Haywood: Haywood History Committee, 2007.

Tremblay, Ghislain. *Ste-Flavie a 150 ans.* Ste-Flavie : Paroisse de Ste-Flavie, 1979.

Grandin, Temple. *Thinking In Pictures: My Life With Autism.* New York: Vintage, 2006.

Grandin, Temple. *DIFFERENT… Not Less.* Arlington: Future Horizons, 2012.

Carrier, Roch. *The Hockey Sweater.* Toronto: Tundra Books, 1999.

Carrier, Roch. *A Happy New Year's Day.* Montreal: Tundra Books, 1991.

Dunn, Lloyd H.. *Exceptional Children in the Schools.* New York: Holt, Rinehart and Winston, 1965.

Gatehouse, Jonathon. *The Instigator: How Gary Bettman Remade The League And Changed The Game Forever*:

Newspaper and Periodical

Winnipeg Free Press

Winnipeg Sun

The Hockey News

The Globe and Mail
The National Post
The Brandon Sun

Reports, Research Papers, and Press Releases

Residences for Retarded in Canada 1966-1967, Prepared by CARC Residential Care Committee, Mrs. R.G. Anglin, March 1967

"Witney Names Two New Medical Superintendents" Provincial Press Release, December 23, 1965

Premier Ed Schreyer's speech at the Manitoba School for Retardates Open House, Sunday, September 26, 1971. Archives of Manitoba, Q27492, EC0030, GR6792

Integrated Services Set for Mental Retardates–Based on Programs Within Community, Provincial Press Release, February 28, 1975

Osborne, John. *The Evolution Of The Canada Assistance Plan*, National Health and Welfare, 1985

Movies

Temple Grandin. Burbank: Home Box Office Films, Inc., 2010

Troyer, Warner. *104-3rd Street: The Kin Glen Home Documentary*. Canadian Broadcasting Corporation, 1967

Websites and Online Resources

www.lesfamilleslanglois.com/ancetres/Noël.html

http:/en.wikipedia.org/wiki/Autism

http://www.autismsocietycanada.ca/understanding-asds/what-are-autism-spectrum-disorders

http://www.autism.org.uk/about-autism/autism-and-asperger-syndrome-an-introduction/what-is-autism.aspx

YouTube.com

http://www.larche.ca/en/jean_vanier/biography

http://www.faithandlight.org/rubriques/haut/actualites/templeton-prize-release-embargo-11-march-1030gmt.pdf

http://www.canadiansocialresearch.net/capjack.htm

Yuhas, Daisy. "Throughout History, Defining Schizophrenia Remains A Challenge (Timeline)". Scientific American Mind (March 2013). Retrieved 2 March 2013.

http://tracksidetreasure.blogspot.ca/2009/11/west-tower-portage-la-prairie-manitoba.html

http://www.special-learning.com/article/full_scale_intelligence_quotient_fsiq

http://ericae.net/eac/eac0141.htm

http://www.stanfordbinet.net

http://www.faithandlight.org/rubriques/haut/about-us/history

http://www.tvarchive.ca/database/19188/archie_and_his_friends/details/

http://www.wrha.mb.ca/prog/surgery/gamma_knife/

http://cfl.uploads.mrx.ca/wpg/downloads/downloads/2013/05/yourguidetoinvestorsgroupfield-final2013050700.pdf

http://www.bluebombers.com/cory-mcdiarmid

http://en.wikipedia.org/wiki/Manitoba_Marathon

http://www.thehockeynews.com/blog/the-worlds-best-hockey-fan-it-might-just-be-the-winnipeg-jets-dancin-gabe/

http://mytoba.ca/voices/dancing-gabe-belongs-in-manitoba-sports-hall-of-fame/

http://tomandlarry.ca/dancing-gabe-larrys-lady-butt-and-freeze-your-pants/

http://www.winnipegbusstories.com/2011/06/dancing-gabe-winnipeg-hero.html

http://www.judsonlaipply.com/evolution-of-dance/

http://brendagorlick.ca/Gorlick_Bio.htm

https://www.smd.mb.ca/smd-services/news-and-media/read,article/48/smd-puts-best-foot-forward-all-abilties-dance-program

http://www.larche.ca/publications/the_beginnings_of_larche_1964-1968.pdf

http://v1.theglobeandmail.com/v5/content/features/focus/boyinthemoon/part1/chapter4/

PHOTO CREDITS

Photo of Dr. Glen Lowther courtesy of Dr. Lowther.

Photo of CP3120 by the CP Train Station in Portage la Prairie (2007) by Steve Boyko, traingeek.ca.

Photo of Gabe and Premier Gary Doer courtesy of Kent Paterson, YMCA.

Photo/Selfie of Gabe and Mason Juras by Mason Juras. Reproduced with permission from Mason's father, Gordon Juras.

Photo of Dancing Gabe and Prime Minister Stephen Harper by Jeff Miller. Reproduced with permission from 100 Acre Woods Photography, Winnipeg, MB.

Colour Dancing With Celebrities photo by Richard Marquez, Where to Look Photography. Reproduced with permission from the Society for Manitobans with Disabilities.

Photo of Gabe carrying the Pan Am torch by Joe Bryksa. Reproduced with permission from the *Winnipeg Free Press*.

Dancing With Celebrities photo in Chapter 23 taken from the Shaw TV video on YouTube (https://www.youtube.com/watch?v=OeIABVrWtDQ).

Unless indicated in the captions, all other photos are courtesy of the Langlois family or by the author.